Going Forward on Your Knees

Going Forward on Your Knees

A NEW BIOGRAPHY

Lessons from the life of Hudson Taylor

Joanna E. Williamson

Authentic

This edition first published 2011 by Authentic Media Limited
PO Box 6326, Bletchley, Milton Keynes MK1 9GG.
authenticmedia.co.uk

British Library Cataloguing in Publication Data

A catalogue record for this book is available from the
British Library

ISBN 978-1-85078-718-1

Cover design by Huw Tyler, Share Creative
Printed and bound by Lightning Source

For Truett Cathy and friends at Chick-fil-A, and my wonderful, visionary husband Mark

Contents

Preface – One Rock International

This book is part of a series that has been developed by One Rock International; each book is a biography of a different missionary leader. One Rock International is passionate about empowering Christian leaders to find and fulfil God's vision for their lives, and so further his kingdom in places and ministry contexts all over the globe.

Throughout the history of Christianity, there have been countless examples of missionary leaders who allowed God to do incredible things through them. However, many of their stories and lives are unknown to this generation. These books aim to remind us of all that God has done through individuals in the past, and so give us a greater expectation of what he might do through us in the present and future.

Each book tells the life story of an individual, using many of their own words so we can hear their unique voice. Each aims to be packed with information, brief in length, and readable in style.

At the end of each chapter there are learning summaries, with key points so that leaders in the twenty-first century can learn from these people of history. They are grouped into the four curriculum areas that One Rock resources people in: Spiritual Formation, Discerning

Vision, Leadership Skills and Mission Skills. Each of these is denoted by the following icons:

 Spiritual Formation

 Discerning Vision

 Leadership Skills

 Mission Skills

We hope these books challenge, inspire and inform your leadership for Jesus. For more information and resources, visit www.onerockinternational.com

Foreword

I have a concern. It is a concern shared by others. As I look around, indeed as I look at my own life, I am concerned by the all too often shallow nature of our love for Christ and our love for those who do not know him. We are distracted. We have, certainly in the West, all we need. We are comfortable. Christianity is comfortable. We have no need to go deep with God. It is warm in the shallows.

A pastor I deeply respect once urged me to read biographies of those men and women who have gone before us, men and women whom God used to great effect in this needy world. I have sought to heed that advice.

I am pleased therefore, to say a few words as you prepare to read the pages ahead of you. Hudson Taylor was unquestionably a man used by God to great effect. Multitudes of Chinese believers would testify to that today, and here Joanna Williamson seeks to present, clearly and concisely, why that is so. However, prepare to be challenged! Hudson Taylor is of a different era, a different world, a world where the call to overseas mission bears little comparison to such a call today. No aeroplanes, no email, precious little medicine or technology. No wonder we read within these pages of a man, often amid horrendous trials, desperately seeking to go deeper with God.

I am not surprised that Joanna elected to write about Hudson Taylor for her first book. Having known Joanna for some time, I am aware of her hunger to go deep with God, and in this Hudson Taylor has certainly been an inspiration. As such, one of the beauties of this book is Joanna allowing Hudson Taylor to tell the story himself. It helps the reader get 'inside the man' and it would be difficult not to be inspired, and more importantly, moved to action.

Joanna has weaved together this snapshot of Hudson Taylor's life in a style that is engaging and accessible to all. It is an inspiring read and with application points at the end of each chapter, this biography seeks to be more than just a good book to pass the time!

Whether you are in Christian leadership, involved with some form of ministry, or simply wanting to know God better, you will appreciate this read. The life of Hudson Taylor speaks to all and Joanna carefully draws out qualities pertaining to your walk with Christ, wherever you find yourself at the moment.

Aside from those of more mature Christian years, I hope that Joanna's concise and thought provoking approach will encourage young readers to dig into the lives of those who have gone before us. Let us not forget that Hudson Taylor, like so many of his contemporaries, was gripped by the call of God at a young age! If you are of later years, why not pass your read copy on to a young person? Who knows how God may use these pages to change history?

As an evangelist I am humbled by the life of Hudson Taylor. The title of this book says it all. How easy it is to talk about love for God! Talk is easy. As you read these pages, may the Lord stir you to a greater hunger for him.

Rev. Martin Durham
Director, Kerygma180

Introduction

Why should you read this book?
Because if you are not standing on the shoulders of giants
you are tiny. Hudson Taylor was a giant . . .
How tall are you?

I am lonely, disappointed, bruised. I am tired of superficiality and pretending, of not seeing fruit from my striving, of always having to work harder, and proving (even if only to myself) I am not a failure. I am a Christian leader.

Who was Hudson Taylor?

A romantic, who persevered through the darkest valleys, who left a mission society because it was in debt, who was weak in his health, without ordination, and as someone said, 'called by no one, connected to no one, and recognised by no one as a minister of the Gospel. Fanatical, undependable, diseased in body.'[1] He constantly endured months of travelling, followed by months of recovering from poor health. All this with the unpredictable rhythms of Chinese history always in the background, at times like roaring dark seas full of darkness and death, and at other times ebbing away, still and smooth. Such were the doors of mission, closing and opening unexpectedly.

It is the details of his life that spoke to me; the little, seemingly insignificant details that touched and remoulded my way of thinking about service, and life in general. For it is there, in the seemingly boring, grey and ordinary days, where character is formed. This book is a testimony of the strength God manifested out of the weakness of people. Two books about the life of Hudson Taylor had an impact on me especially: *Hudson Taylor in Early Years: The Growth of the Soul* and *Hudson Taylor and the China Inland Mission: The Growth of the Work of God*. In telling the story I have used these two extensively. The testimony of Hudson Taylor has encouraged me, made me a better leader and saved my ministry from the shipwreck of discouragement.

There are many people who possess a vision of (personal) evolution yet seem to lack the will for it. They want, and believe it is possible, to skip over the discipline, to find an easy shortcut to sainthood. Often they attempt to attain it by simply imitating the superficialities of saints, retiring to the desert or taking up carpentry. Some even believe that by such imitation they have really become saints and prophets, and are unable to acknowledge that they are still children and face the painful fact that they must start at the beginning and go through the middle.[2]

Hudson Taylor once said, 'I have found that there are three stages in every great work of God; first it is impossible, then it is difficult, then it is done.'[3] It is this middle bit, the 'difficult' stage, that requires staying power, and a close intimacy with God, to move us on to the 'done'. It is going through the middle that puts many of us off. It is humdrum and ordinary. Hudson Taylor teaches us discipline will bring us not only to the fulfilment of vision, but will help us in the darkest times of self-doubt and disappointment. This is why it is so important we learn to go forward on our knees. I hope this book will help you 'go through the middle' with integrity, and set you on fire.

1

It Is Finished, It Has Just Begun

1832–49

James Hudson Taylor, known to all simply as Hudson Taylor, was born 21 May 1832 in Cheapside, Barnsley. He would grow up and go on to become one of the greatest missionaries the church had ever seen, and would have a profound effect on the scope of the work of God in China.

Childhood

He grew up under the watchful eye of hardworking and godly parents, and shared the joys of his simple yet nourishing childhood years with two sisters. It was at home where he learned about discipline, the need for usefulness and cleanliness, and the value of prayer and study. From an overheard fireplace conversation here he first learned about the needs of mission in China.

Catching something of the fire of his own father, and his desire for the evangelization of China, he was heard to say that when he grew up he wanted to be a missionary in China. However, Hudson Taylor's health was poor. As much as his parents wanted his wish to come true, they were also very much aware their son might not be able to make it.

Yet what God planted in his heart at a young age never left him. Later on, he was hit by the struggles many teenagers go through. School was difficult; he could not attend regularly due to poor health, and missed a lot of lessons. On top of that, he was trying to work out his own salvation, but as he was trying to do it in his own strength he failed over and over again. Of his own striving, he said:

> Often had I tried to make myself a Christian, and failing of course in such efforts, I began to think that for some reason or other I could not be saved, and that the best I could do was to take my fill of this world, as there was no hope for me beyond the grave. While in this state of mind I came in contact with persons holding sceptical and infidel views, and quickly accepted their teachings, only too thankful for some hope of escape from the doom which if my parents were right and the Bible true awaited the ungodly.[4]

Hudson Taylor was looking for a true expression of Christianity. He saw too may lukewarm Christians. If he was to follow Jesus he wanted to follow wholeheartedly. But just as it was true for Paul the Apostle, Hudson Taylor could not 'kick against the goads forever'. Soon God touched his conscience in a way he could not ignore.

> It may seem strange, but I have often felt thankful for this time of scepticism. The inconsistencies of Christian people who while professing to believe the Bible were yet content

to live just as they would if there were no such book, had been one of the strongest arguments of my sceptical companions, and I frequently felt at that time, and said, that if I pretended to believe the Bible I would at any rate attempt to live by it, putting it fairly to the test, and if it failed to prove true and reliable, would throw it overboard altogether. These views I retained when the Lord was pleased to bring me to Himself. And I think I may say that since then I have put God's Word to the test. Certainly it has never failed me. I have never had reason to regret the confidence I have placed in its promises, or to deplore following the guidance I have found in its directions.[5]

Conversion

His conversion was an amazing answer to prayer. No wonder that later on in his life he relied on prayer so much. His very motto was: *to move people, through God, by prayer*. One day, a touch bored, he walked into his father's library and picked up a gospel tract. The story reads best in his own words.

And now let me tell you how God answered the prayers of my mother and of my beloved sister, now Mrs Broomhall, for my conversion.

On a day I can never forget . . . my dear mother being absent from home, I had a holiday, and in the afternoon looked through my father's library to find some book with which to while away the unoccupied hours. Nothing attracting me, I turned over a basket of pamphlets and selected from amongst them a Gospel tract that looked interesting, saying to myself: 'There will be a story at the commencement and a sermon or moral at the close. I will take the former and leave the latter for those who like it.'

I sat down to read the book in an utterly unconcerned state of mind, believing indeed at the time that if there were any salvation it was not for me, and with a distinct intention to put away the tract as soon as it should seem prosy. I may say that it was not uncommon in those days to call conversion 'becoming serious'; and judging by the faces of some of its professors it appeared to be a very serious matter indeed! Would it not be well if the people of God had always tell-tale faces, evincing the blessings and gladness of salvation so clearly that unconverted people might have to call conversion 'becoming joyful' instead of 'becoming serious'?

Little did I know at that time what was going on in the heart of my dear mother, seventy or eighty miles away. She rose from the dinner table that afternoon with an intense yearning for the conversion of her boy; and feeling that, absent from her home and having more leisure than she could otherwise secure, a special opportunity was afforded her of pleading with God on my behalf. She went to her room and turned the key in the door, resolved not to leave the spot until her prayers were answered. Hour after hour that dear mother pleaded, until at length she could pray no longer, but was constrained to praise God for that which His Spirit taught her had already been accomplished, the conversion of her only son.

I in the meantime had been led in the way I have mentioned to take up this little tract, and while reading it was struck with the phrase: 'the finished work of Christ.'

Why does the author use this expression? I questioned. Why not say the atoning or propitiatory work of Christ? Immediately the words 'it is finished' suggested themselves to my mind. 'What was finished?' And at once replied, 'A full and perfect atonement and satisfaction for sin. The debt was paid for our sins, and not for ours only, but also for the sins of the whole world.'

Then came the further thought, 'if the whole work was finished and the whole debt paid, what is there left for me to do? And with this dawned the joyful conviction, as light was flashed into my soul by the Holy Spirit, that there was nothing in the world to be done but to fall down on one's knees and, accepting this Saviour and His salvation, praise Him for evermore.

Thus while my dear mother was praising God on her knees in her chamber, I was praising Him in the old warehouse to which I had gone alone to read at my leisure this little book. Several days elapsed ere I ventured to make my beloved sister the confidante of my joy, and then only after she had promised not to tell anyone of my soul-secret. When Mother returned a fortnight later I was the first to meet her at the door and to tell her I had such glad news to give. I can almost feel that dear mother's arms round my neck as she pressed me to her heart and said: 'I know, my boy. I have been rejoicing for a fortnight in the glad tidings you have to tell.'

'Why,' I asked in surprise, 'has Amelia broken her promise? She said she would tell no one.' My dear mother assured me that it was not from any human source she had learned the tidings, and went on to tell the incident mentioned above. You will agree with me that it would be strange indeed if I were not a believer in the power of prayer. Nor was this all. Sometime after, I picked up a pocket-book exactly like my own, and thinking it was mine, opened it. The lines that caught my eye were an entry in the little diary belonging to my sister, to the effect that she would give herself daily to prayer until God should answer in the conversion of her brother. One month later the Lord was pleased to turn me from darkness into light.

Brought up in such a circle and saved under such circumstances, it was perhaps natural that from the commencement of my Christian life I was left to feel that the promises were very real, and that prayer was in sober matter of fact transacting business with God whether on one's own behalf or on the behalf of those for whom one sought His blessing.

It Is Finished, It Has Just Begun

Key learning points

Spiritual Formation

Spiritual Formation starts at home. Hudson Taylor learned the importance of discipline, study and faithfulness in small things from his parents. No matter whether good or bad, our early years and upbringing shape and influence us.

Realize you cannot make yourself a Christian. We cannot be saved by trying to do better. Faith in Christ and his finished work on the cross is what makes us a Christian.

Do not be afraid of seasons of doubt. Hudson Taylor was not satisfied with what he had seen from nominal Christianity. He knew there was more. He also clung even closer to God in the times of questioning. He made a decision to follow him wholeheartedly.

Believe in the power of prayer. Hudson Taylor came to Christ through the prayer of his mother. Prayer remained a powerful force and a primary strategy throughout his life.

Discerning Vision

Great visions start with small seeds. God can place his desires in our hearts even from a very young age. The beginning of Hudson Taylor's vision for China dates back to his childhood.

2

Going All Lengths with God

1849–50

Having resolved to give his life to Jesus, Hudson Taylor still had spiritual struggles. Eventually, he prevailed through temptations, battles and discouragements. He emerged with a clear sense of the call of God on his life.

After his conversion, though not immediately, came the call. The conversion, though powerful, was not the final work of God in Hudson Taylor. The work had only just begun, and during his whole life Hudson Taylor was to long for more and more of God. All opposition made him press on closer to God's heart. He tasted something of the goodness of God, and he resolved never throughout his whole life to settle for anything less than God's perfect will. God would continue to enlarge the territory of his ministry and the scope of his responsibility. His character and calling would be tested on a regular basis, and there would never be an end to the opposition he faced – but God's faithfulness would never run dry either.

There are four important principles we can draw from his life at that time. Two preceded his call and two followed.

Principle of surrender

With conversion came the need to surrender his whole life to God.

Well do I remember that occasion . . . how in the gladness of my heart I poured out my soul before God, and again confessing my grateful love to Him who had done everything for me – who had saved me when I had given up all hope and even desire for salvation – I besought Him to give me some work for Him, as an outlet for love and gratitude; some self-denying service, no matter what it might be, however trying or however trivial; something with which He would be pleased and that I might do for Him who had done so much for me. Well do I remember, as in unreserved consecration I put myself, my life, my friends, my all upon the altar, the deep solemnity that came over my soul with the assurance that my offering was accepted. The presence of God became unutterably real and blessed, and I well remember . . . stretching myself on the ground, and lying there before Him with unspeakable awe and unspeakable joy. For what service I was accepted I knew not. But a deep consciousness that I was not my own took possession of me, which has never since been effaced.[7]

Principle of choice

Then, soon after, came the calling, and with the calling he had to make a choice. Later on, Dr and Mrs Howard Taylor, his future son and daughter-in-law, wrote about this time:

He recognized that he was saved to serve, and that a work was waiting for which a life of inner victory and power would be essential. He had had his unsatisfactory experiences, and deeply knew how little a man has for others who is not himself walking at liberty within. During his sceptical days he had seen that the only logical position for the Christian is to go all lengths with God.[8]

The inner conflict lasted for several months. There were times of victory and times of defeat. 'Prayer was an effort and the Bible devoid of interest.'[9] The surrender to God had brought much joy and peace to his heart, and had opened his eyes to the needs around him, but it also made him become more aware of his own sinfulness, and his personal struggle with sin.

He found himself yielding to temptation, ease-indulged, and often disinclined for private prayer and study of the Word of God.

At such times two courses are open to the perplexed and troubled soul. One is to abandon the ideal, and gradually sink down to a low-level Christian life in which there is neither joy nor power. The other is just to go on with the Lord, and because of his 'exceeding great and precious promises' to claim complete deliverance not from the guilt only, but from the mastery of sin, just to go on with the Lord, trusting His strength and faithfulness to pardon, loose and cleanse, to sanctify us wholly, and to make our own every blessing promised in the eternal covenant.[10]

Call

After Hudson Taylor surrendered and made the choice of 'going all lengths with God' a clear call came. Days of hunger and pangs for holiness would persist throughout his life, but he also experienced a renewed sense of victory over sin. He took his eyes off himself and looked to God: he showed him the way ahead.

Never shall I forget the feeling that came over me then. Words can never describe it. I felt I was in the presence of God, entering into covenant with the Almighty. I felt as though I wished to withdraw my promise, but I could not. Something seemed to say 'your prayer is answered, your conditions are accepted.' And from that time the conviction never left me that I was called to China.[11]

'"From that hour," [his] mother wrote, "his mind was made up. His pursuits and studies were all engaged in with reference to this object, and whatever difficulties presented themselves his purpose never wavered."'[12]

Historical Background

In 1834 the Protestant Mission in China consisted of exactly seven persons. There was Robert Morrison, who had come to China in 1807 for the London Missionary Society; E Coleman Bridgman who had arrived in 1829 for the American Board of Commissioners for Foreign Missions; Karl Gutzlaff, a

German once sponsored by Netherlands Missionary Society, now on his own; Edwin Stevens of the American Seaman's Friends Society; two more Americans, S. Wells Williams and Ira Tracy, sent out by the American Board; and one single Chinese, Liang Afa. One missionary had called it a 'feeble band ridiculous in the world's eyes, going to convert China', and facing one might add, difficulties so insurmountable that seemingly nothing could cut a path through them save an act of God. (They included housing, health issues, lack of money, opposition and ridicule, language issues and war.) China was almost unknown to the western world. Just five ports – Canton, Amoy, Fuchow, Ningpo and Shanghai – were opened by the Treaty of Nanking in 1842.

Principle of cost

It seemed to me highly probable . . . that the work to which I was thus called might cost my life. China was not open then as it is now. Few missionary societies had representatives there, and few books on the subject were accessible to me.

I learned, however, that a minister in my native town possessed a copy of Midhurst's *China*, and calling upon him ventured to ask a loan of the book. This he kindly granted, inquiring why I wished to read it. I told him that God had called me to spend my life in missionary service in that land. 'And how do you propose to go there?' he enquired.

I answered that I did not at all know; that it seemed to me probable that I should need to go as the Twelve and the Seventy had done in Judea, go without purse or scrip, relying on Him who had sent me to supply all my need.

Kindly placing his hand on my shoulder, the minister replied, 'Ah my boy, as you grow older you will become wiser than that. Such an idea would do very well in the days when Christ Himself was on earth, but not now.'

I have grown older since then, but not wiser. I am more convinced that if we were to take the directions of our Master and the assurance He gave to his first disciples more fully as our guide, we should find them just as suited to our times as to those in which they were originally given.[13]

Medhurst's book on China emphasized the value of medical missions, and this directed Hudson Taylor to study to become a doctor.

Principle of usefulness

Oliver Wendell Holmes said, 'Some people are so heavenly minded that they are of no earthly use.' This was not so with Hudson Taylor, who always longed to be useful, understanding that God calls us to friendship *and* to function. He continued to wait on God for guidance; continued to prepare himself to be a missionary. He believed the door could open at any minute, and he wanted to be ready.

I began to take more exercise in the open air to strengthen my general health. My feather bed was soon dispensed with, and as many other comforts as possible, in order to prepare for a rougher sort of life. I began also to do what Christian work was in my power, in the way of tract distribution, Sunday-school teaching, and visiting the poor and sick as opportunity afforded.[14]

Sometime later he wrote to George Pearse of the Chinese Evangelisation Society (CES).

I have devoted myself to missionary work in China in obedience I believe to His call, and am at present studying medicine and surgery that I may have more opportunities of usefulness and perhaps be able to support myself when I am there. This, however, I leave in His hands, believing that if I seek first the Kingdom of God and His righteousness all these things shall be 'added' according to His promise. Any suggestions you may be able to give me as to means for promoting the cause or fitting myself for more extensive usefulness would be thankfully received by – Yours in our Risen Lord, J. H. Taylor.[15]

Little was known about China, and obtaining any resources for learning the language was difficult. Yet God's call upon our lives makes us unstoppable, and his energy and creativity rubs off on us. That was certainly true when it came to the study of Chinese. The only text in Chinese Hudson Taylor had was the Gospel of Luke, and this became his handbook. With no dictionary, but with the help of his cousin, he was able to work out 500 characters.

We find a short verse in the English version, and then look out a dozen or more (also in English) that have one word in common with it. We then turn up the first verse in Chinese, and search through all the others for some character in common that seems to stand for the English word. Then we look all through the Chinese Gospel for this same character in different connections. And if in every case we find the same word in the English version, we copy the character in ink into our dictionary, adding the meaning in pencil. Afterwards, if further acquaintance shows it to be the true meaning, we ink that over also. At first we made slow progress, but now we can work much faster, as with few exceptions we know all the most common characters. I have begun to get up at five in the morning, and so find it necessary to go to bed early at night. I must study if I mean to go to China. I am fully decided to go, and am making every preparation I can. I intend to rub up my Latin, to learn Greek and the rudiments of Hebrew, and get as much general information as possible.[16]

Disappointments

However, the enemy never sleeps and always looks for opportunities to discourage and derail us; to discredit our ministry and make us lose focus. One of the most respected and well known missionaries in China at that time was Karl Gutzlaff.

Gutzlaff's piety was deep and real, his schemes were large and his optimism unbounded. He was a man of unusual gifts, and as Interpreter to the British Government in Hong Kong occupied a position of influence. So great was his enthusiasm for the spread of the Gospel that he had risked his life repeatedly in daring attempts to reach the interior, as well as in voyages along the entire cost.[17]

Later on, great dishonesty amongst Gutzlaff's native workers was uncovered, and people in England were deeply disappointed. A lot of impressive testimonies relating to the evangelization of certain areas were lies told by so-called 'evangelists', who, instead of doing the work of God, smoked opium in nearby caves and went about making up statistics and stories of conversions. Gutzlaff was not aware of what was happening, and soon after the exposure he passed away. Many said he died of a broken heart.

This episode had an extremely negative impact on the attitude towards mission in China. However, it inspired Hudson Taylor to persevere. He was struggling with disappointment in another area. Her name was Marianne Vaughan, and she was his sister Amelia's teacher. She came to visit the family for Christmas and he fell head-over-heels in love with her. In one of his many letters he wrote:

Dear Amelia, remember me in all your prayers. Never did I feel a greater need of watchfulness and prayer than at present. Praise be God, I know that the blood of Jesus cleanses from all sin, but I feel my own weakness, my own nothingness. Without His aid I cannot stand for one moment, but I look to the Strong for strength, and though he that trusteth in man shall be disappointed, blessed are all they that put their trust in the Lord. I realise this blessedness. I feel that I can trust Him with all my concerns. I can and do 'praise Him for all that is past, and trust Him for all that's to come'. He has promised to withhold 'no good thing' from those that walk uprightly. I do love Him, and am determined to devote myself, body, soul and spirit, to His work.

Pray for me, dear Amelia, that I may have more of the mind of Christ; that I may be guided in all things by His Holy Spirit and made very useful. Pray for the cause of God and expect an answer. Pray on for China. . . .[18]

He had doubts about the relationship and had difficulty imagining how it would work from the very beginning. He hoped Marianne was the right one for him; but she hoped he would change his mind about going to China, and instead find himself a proper job. Many months of prayer and waiting followed. However, for Hudson Taylor, his desire to serve China was only intensifying.

I have stronger desire than ever to go to China. That land is ever in my thoughts. Think of it – three hundred and sixty million souls, without God or hope in the world. Think of more than twelve millions of our fellow-creatures dying every year without any of the consolations of the Gospel . . . Barnsley including the Common has only fifteen thousand inhabitants. Imagine what it would be if all there were to die in twelve months. Yet in China hundreds are dying, year by year, for every man, woman and child in Barnsley. Poor neglected China! Scarcely anyone cares about it. And that immense country, containing nearly a fourth of the human race, is left in ignorance and darkness.[19]

Preparations

With no openings for him to go, with hardly any materials on China or resources for language learning, and with no idea how he would go about raising the necessary funding, he persisted in getting ready. Whilst laying his love for Marianne before God, he took hold of present opportunities, working with the poor in his local community. He used to say, 'The voyage across the oceans does not make any man a soul winner.'[20]

A letter to Mr Pearse gives more details of his personal life.

Some of the reasons that make me think, nay, make me sure (for I have no doubt on the matter) that I am truly converted to God are as follows:

The things I used formerly to delight in now give me no pleasure, while reading the Word, prayer and the means of grace, which were formerly distasteful to me, are now my delight.

I know I have passed from death unto life because I love the brethren. The Spirit of God bears direct witness with my spirit that I am His child. My mind is kept in perfect peace because I trust in Him. And I feel no doubt that should I be called hence, when this earthly tabernacle is dissolved I have a building of God, a house not made with hands, eternal in the heavens. I feel I am but a stranger here. Heaven is my home . . . I know that in myself there is nothing that can merit Heaven. I am a poor, helpless, hell-deserving sinner. But in Him all fullness dwells. I am, praised be God, a sinner saved by grace.

My age will be nineteen on the 21st of May 1851. Of course I am unmarried.

As to the general state of my health, I have never had any serious illness, but cannot be called robust. I have never been better than at present, and intend to take more care of my health than I have previously done, having often neglected exercises for weeks together in order to have more time for study.

My occupation has been, since Christmas 1845, with the exception of nine months spent in the bank, that of assistant to my father, who is a chemist and druggist.

My education was carried on at home until I was eleven years of age. Then I went to school, and continued there until I was thirteen, when the master resigning without arranging for efficient substitute, I left at the Christmas vacation and came into the shop. Beside the regular routine of study, I worked at Latin, Euclid and Algebra, in which I took great interest. Since then I have had access to a tolerably good library, and have acquired the rudiments of Greek as well as of Anatomy and Physiology.

With regard to denominational views: at first I joined the Wesleyan Methodists, as my parents and friends were members of that body. But not being able to reconcile the late proceedings with the doctrines and precepts of Holy Scripture, I withdrew, and am at present united to the branch Society.

Apologising for thus intruding upon your time – I remain, dear Sir, yours in our beloved Redeemer, James Hudson Taylor.[21]

Going All Lengths with God

Key learning points

Spiritual Formation

Surrender is key to hearing God's voice. Putting everything on the altar is an important step in choosing to follow God.

Choices are inevitable. Hudson Taylor came to a place of choice, the 'valley of decision'. Make a choice to 'go all lengths with God'.

Do not be put off by a continuous battle with sin. Continue to develop a greater love for God, and trust him to help you overcome temptation.

Discerning Vision

Calculate the cost. Hudson Taylor knew that his vision could cost him his life, and would require huge personal sacrifice, but he was determined to carry it through.

Know that there is a role for you to play in God's plan. Hudson Taylor longed to be used by God. He studied medicine in order to be more useful when in the mission field.

Seek advice. Once he had discerned God's call on his life, Hudson Taylor wrote to the Chinese Evangelisation Society to ask for their wisdom. Learn from those already working in the area of your call, rather than seeking to do things alone.

Leadership Skills

Trust God to provide. Do not be idle in seeking finance, but remember that 'God's work, done in God's way, never lacks God's provision.'[22]

Prepare. Hudson Taylor taught himself Chinese in his spare time, whilst also studying medicine. Take the little steps possible today to prepare you for the fulfilment of your vision tomorrow.

3

A Living Epistle

1850–54

Taking the opportunity to be an assistant to a doctor, Hudson Taylor set off for Hull, and then, to continue his education, went to London. He was nineteen years old when he left home, never to come back except for a few short visits. This time of work, study and ongoing spiritual preparation spanned three years – from 1850, the year he went to Hull, through to September 1853, the month he sailed to China for the first time.

Preparation for ministry

Much happened during those three years: heartbreak over a relationship; a strengthening of his call; a life-threatening illness; and a new level of spirituality.

It was also a time of massive personal change, as living away from home greatly increased his self-knowledge. He constantly thought of China, and how he could best prepare for it, but his time at the surgery provided little opportunity to immerse himself in anything else but work. He continually thought of Marianne too, and worried how it would be resolved. Would he have enough money to provide for her? Would she come to China with him?

From this period we learn much about his steward-ship of money, and his constant hunger to grow more in faith; a hunger not in any way diminished by his busy life. At this time he was heard to say, 'A little thing is a little thing, but faithfulness in little things is a great thing.'[23]

Before leaving Barnsley my attention was drawn to the subject of setting apart the first fruits of all one's increase and a certain proportion of one's possessions for the service of the Lord. It seemed to me desirable to study the question, Bible in hand, and in this way I was led to the determination to set apart not less than one-tenth of whatever money I might earn or become possessed of, for the Lord. After much thought and prayer, I was led to leave the comfortable home and pleasant circle in which I resided, and engage a little lodging in the suburbs, a sit-ting room and bedroom in one. Undertaking to board myself, I was thus enabled to tithe the whole of my income; and while one felt the change a good deal, it was attended with no small blessing. More time was given in my solitude to the study of the Word of God, to visiting the poor and to evangelistic work on Sunday evening than would otherwise have been the case. Brought into contact in this way with many who were in distress, I soon saw the privilege of still further economizing, and found it possible to give away much more than I had at first intended.

I learned, too, that the period of His return for His people was not revealed, and that it was their privilege, from day to day and from hour to hour, to live as men who wait for the Lord; that thus living it was immaterial, so to speak, whether He should or should not come at any particular hour, the important thing being to be so ready for Him as to be able, whether He might appear, to give an account of one's stewardship with joy, and not with grief.

The effect of this blessed hope was a thoroughly practical one. It led me to look carefully through my little library to see if there were any books there that were not needed or likely to be of further service, and to examine my small wardrobe, to be quite sure that it contained nothing that I should be sorry to give an account of should the Master come at once. The result was that the library was considerably diminished to the benefit of some poor neighbours, and to the far greater benefit of my own soul, and that I found I had articles of clothing also which might be put to better advantage in other directions.

It has been very helpful to me from time to time through life, as occasion has served, to act again in a similar way; and I have never gone through my house, from basement to attic, with the object in view, without receiving a great accession of spiritual joy and blessing. I believe we are all in danger of accumulating – it may be from thoughtlessness, or from pressure of occupation – things which would be useful to others, while not needed by ourselves, and the retention of which entails loss of blessing. If the whole resources of the Church of God were well utilized, how much more might be accomplished! How many poor might be fed and naked clothed, and to how many of those as yet unreached the Gospel might be carried! Let me advise this line of things as a constant habit of mind, and a profitable course to be practically adopted whether circumstances permit.

Having now the twofold object in view of accustoming myself to endure hardness, and of economizing in order to be able more largely to assist those amongst whom I spent a good deal of time labouring in the Gospel, I soon found that I could live upon very much less than I had previously thought possible. Butter, milk and other luxuries I ceased to use, and found that by living mainly on oatmeal and rice, with occasional variations, a very small sum was sufficient for my needs. In this way I had more than two-thirds of my income available for other purposes, and my experience was that the less I spent on myself and the more I gave to others the fuller of happiness and blessing did my soul become.[24]

The German missionary Lobscheid was visiting London at that point, and it seemed an ideal opportunity for Hudson Taylor to see the big city for the first time and to meet the famous missionary. Though he did enjoy getting to know a group of Christians in Tottenham (the introduction was made by Mr Pearse, the Secretary of the CES, with whom he had already corresponded), he was a little disappointed to hear discouraging words from the great man. Hudson Taylor had curly blond hair, and Lobscheid told him most of the Chinese were still not accustomed to seeing white people, and would, therefore, probably run away from him due to his appearance. (In future years, the opposite would be true, as Hudson Taylor would strive particularly hard to remove all cross-cultural barriers.)

During his time in Hull Hudson Taylor attended meetings of the Plymouth Brethren. In 1852 he read a book by the German missionary George Müller that deeply impacted his life, and would influence the way he organized and led missionary work in the years to come. It was from Müller he learned never to ask for money, always to be debt-free, and to rely on God as provider.

Plymouth Brethren

Also called Open Brethren, the denomination was established in 1820. Strongly missionary in focus, embracing the priesthood of all believers, they believed in the final authority of the Bible on all issues of life and faith. Their more well-known adherents include: Anthony Norris Grove, missionary in Baghdad, 1829; George Müller, who opened orphanages in Bristol; and Jim Elliot, a missionary killed in Ecuador.

For more information about Plymouth Brethren, see *A History of Plymouth Brethren* by William Blair Neatby (available online).

A man of prayer

Because Hudson Taylor strongly believed mission was not just something done abroad, he always looked for opportunities to get involved in local ministries. There were many such opportunities. He visited the most miserable and dangerous quarters in the town, preaching the gospel and ministering to people. He said, 'I try to be a living epistle'; he was beginning to form his life's motto.[25]

To me it was a very grave matter to contemplate going to China, far from all human aid, there to depend upon the living God alone for protection, supplies, and help of every kind. I felt that one's spiritual muscles required strengthening for such an undertaking. There was no doubt that if faith did not fail, God would not fail. But what if one's faith proved insufficient? I had not at that time learned that even 'if we believe not, yet He abideth faithful, He cannot deny Himself.' It was consequently a very serious question to my mind, not whether He was faithful, but whether I had strong enough faith to warrant my embarking in the enterprise set before me.

When I get out to China, I thought to myself, I shall have no claim on anyone for anything. My only claim will be on God. *How important to learn, before leaving England, to move man through God by prayer alone.*[26]

Heartbreak

During all this time of hard work, economizing and praying for China, there was something (or rather, somebody) always at the back of his mind: Marianne. Their love lasted three years and three months. They even got engaged, he still hoping she would change her mind and come with him to China. She did not. Her father was not keen to have his daughter marry a poor, uneducated missionary either. The disappointment left Hudson Taylor disconsolate. The pain the breakdown of this relationship caused, and the discouragement it brought upon him was huge. He loved Marianne, although his feelings did not seem to be reciprocated with the same strength and passion. The disappointment sent him into the depths of depression and disheartened him in his prayer life.

> Alone in the surgery I had a melting season. I was thoroughly softened and humbled and had a wonderful manifestation of the love of God. 'A broken and a contrite heart' He did not despise, but answered my cry for blessing in very deed and truth. May He keep me softened, and thoroughly impress on me the seal of His own nature. Trusting God does not deprive one of feeling or deaden our natural sensibilities, but it enables us to compare our trials with our mercies and to say, 'Yet, notwithstanding, I will rejoice in the Lord, I will joy in the God of my salvation.' It enables us to see . . . the Refiner watching the fire, and be thankful.[27]

It was the spiritual disciplines of prayer, study and community that kept him going.

> For some days I was as wretched as heart could wish. It seemed as if I had no power in prayer nor relish for it; and instead of throwing my care on Him I kept it all to myself until I could endure it no longer. Well, on Sunday I felt no desire to go to the Meeting and was tempted very much. Satan seemed to come in as a flood and I was forced to cry: 'Save, Lord, I perish.' Still Satan suggested, 'You never used to be tried as you have been lately. You can not be in the right path, or God would help and bless you more,' and so on, until I felt inclined to give it all up.

But, thank God, the way of duty is the way of safety. I went to the Meeting after all, as miserable as could be; but did not come away so. One hymn quite cut me to the heart. I was thankful that prayer followed, for I could not keep back my tears. But the load was lighter.

In the afternoon as I was sitting alone in the Surgery I began to reflect on the love of God; His goodness and my return; the number of blessings He has granted me; and how small my trials are compared with those some are called to endure.

He thoroughly softened and humbled me. His love melted my icy, frost-bound soul, and sincerely did I pray for pardon for my ungrateful conduct.

Yes, He has humbled me and shown me what I was, revealing Himself as a present, a very present help in time of trouble. And though He does not deprive me of feelings in my trial, He enables me to sing, 'Yet I will rejoice in the Lord, I will joy in the God of my salvation.' Thus do I rejoice by His Grace, and will rejoice, and praise Him while He lends me breath.[28]

He laid down the attachment at the foot of the cross, never to pick it up again. God would later provide a wonderful companion, but for that he still had to wait several years. Surrendering to the Lord in this area enriched his relationship with God, and renewed his commitment to the vision.

I almost wish I had a hundred bodies. They should all be devoted to my Saviour in the missionary cause. But this is foolishness. I have almost more than I can do to manage one, it is so self-willed, earthly-minded, fleshly. Constantly I am grieving my dear Saviour who shed for me His precious blood, forgetting Him who never has relaxed His watchful care and protection over me from the earlier moment of my existence. I am astonished at the littleness of my gratitude and love for Him and confounded by His long-suffering mercy. Pray for me that I may live more and more to His praise, be more devoted to Him, incessant in labours in His cause, fitted for China, ripened for glory.[29]

We dwell too much on the things that are seen and temporal . . . and far too little on those that are unseen and eternal . . . only let us keep these things in view, and the cares and pleasures of this world will not affect us much . . . oh, my dear Sister, let us live for eternity! Let us seek to be near the throne. What if for this we have to pass, as we undoubtedly shall, through great tribulation? Does He not promise 'I will never leave thee nor forsake thee?' So that we may boldly say: the Lord is my Helper, I will not fear what man shall do unto me. Praise His holy name.[30]

Time in London

Without much planned or certain, and with just a few pounds in his pocket, he set off for London for the next stage of preparation. London afforded an excellent opportunity for the study of medicine, and the CES (which was based there) offered to cover his fees. He first stayed with his uncle Benjamin Hudson, renting a simple attic room. The hospital was located in Whitechapel, about four miles from his accommodation.

He walked every day, no matter the weather, as he could not afford the omnibus fare. He ate only brown bread and apples.

To lessen expenses I shared a room with a cousin, four miles from the hospital, providing my own board; and after various experiments I found that the most economical way was to live almost exclusively on brown bread and water. Thus I was able to make the means that God gave me last as long as possible. Some of my expenses I could not diminish, but my board was largely in my own control. A large two penny loaf of brown bread, purchased daily on my long walk from the hospital, furnished me with supper and breakfast; and on this diet with a few apples for lunch I managed to walk eight or nine miles a day, besides being a good deal on foot attending the practice of the hospital.[31]

Saved from death

Hudson Taylor had never been strong in his health, and the poor diet and daily long walks did not help. Then there were the hazards of working in a hospital.

While sewing together some sheets of paper on which to take notes of lectures, I accidently pricked the first finger of my right hand, and in a few moments forgot all about it. The next day at the hospital I continued dissecting as before. The body was that of a person who had died of fever, and was more than usually disagreeable and dangerous. I need scarcely say that those of us who were at work upon it dissected with special care, knowing that the slightest scratch might cost our lives. Before morning was far advanced I began to feel weary and while going through the surgical wards at noon was obliged to run out, being suddenly very sick – a most unusual circumstance with me, as I took but little food and nothing that could disagree with me. After feeling faint for some time, a draught of cold water revived me and I was able to rejoin the students.

I became more and more unwell however, and during an afternoon lecture on surgery found it impossible to hold the pencil and continue taking notes. By the time the next lecture was over, my whole arm and right side were full of pain and I was both looking and feeling very ill.

Finding that I could not resume work, I went into the dissecting room to bind up the portion I was engaged upon and put away my apparatus, and said to the demonstrator, who was a skilful surgeon:

'I cannot think what has come over me,' describing the symptoms.

'Why?' said he, 'what has happened is clear enough. You must have cut yourself in dissecting, and you know that this is a case of malignant fever.'

I assured him that I had been most careful and was quite certain that I had no cut or scratch.

'Well,' he replied, 'you certainly must have had one'; and he closely scrutinised my hand to find it, in vain.

All at once it occurred to me that I had pricked my finger the night before and I asked him if it were possible that a prick from a needle at that time could have been still unclosed. His opinion was that this was probably the cause of trouble, and he advised me to get a hansom, drive home as fast as I could and arrange my affairs forthwith: 'For' said he, 'you are a dead man.'

My first thought was one of sorrow that I could not go to China; but very soon came the feeling, 'Unless I am greatly mistaken, I have work to do in China and shall not die.' I was glad, however to take the opportunity of speaking to my medical friend, who was a confirmed sceptic, of the joy that the prospect of soon being with my Master gave me, telling him at the same time that I did not think I should die, as unless I were much mistaken I had work to do in China, and if so, however severe the struggle, I must be brought through.

'That is all very well' he answered, 'but get a hansom and drive home as fast as you can. You have no time to lose, for you will soon be incapable of winding up your affairs.'

I smiled a little at the idea of driving home in a hansom, for by this time my means were too exhausted to allow of such a proceeding, and I set out to walk the distance if possible. Before long, however, my strength gave way, and I felt it was no use to attempt to reach home by walking. Availing myself of an omnibus from Whitechapel Church to Farrington Street, and another from Farmington Street onwards, I reached, in great suffering, the neighbourhood of Soho Square behind which I lived. On going into the house I got some hot water from the servant, and charging her very earnestly – literally as a dying man – to accept eternal life as the gift of God through Jesus Christ, I bathed my hand and lanced the finger, hoping to let out some of the poisoned blood. The pain was very severe. I fainted away and was so long unconscious that when I came to myself I found I had been carried to bed.

An uncle of mine who lived at hand had come in, and sent for his own medical man, an assistant surgeon at the Westminster Hospital. I assured my uncle that medical help would be of no service to me, and that I did not wish to go to the expense involved. He quieted me on this score, however, saying that he had sent for his own doctor and that the bill would be charged to himself. When the surgeon came and learned all particulars, he said:

'Well if you have been living moderately you may pull through, but if you have been going in for beer and that sort of thing there is no manner of chance for you.'

I thought that if sober living was to do anything, few could have a better chance, as little but bread and water had been my diet for a good while past. I told him I had lived abstemiously and found that it helped me to study.

'But now' he said 'you must keep up your strength, for it will be a pretty hard struggle.' And he ordered me a bottle of port wine every day and as many chops as I could consume. Again I smiled inwardly, having no means for the purchase of such luxuries. This difficulty however was also met by my kind uncle, who sent me at once all that was needed . . .[32]

Recovery was very slow, and he was depleted spiritually too; months of hard work and poor diet were exacting their toll on him.

Six months later, in spring 1853, he started to work at a doctors' surgery in the City. Every area of his life seemed difficult: finances, workload and studies – and in the midst of all these, the constant call of China, and how to fulfil it.

All of us go through times of disillusionment. We think: if only I had this or that, if only this would work out for me, I would be so much more fulfilled, and would be able to accomplish so much more. There will always be obstacles: the secret is to accomplish things despite all of the attendant difficulties.

The door opens

Seasons in the lives of Christians can change overnight, and God can turn situations around completely unexpectedly. So it was that China opened up her gates a little more. The Taiping Rebellion, which later became a corrupt political movement, covered China with darkness and fear – the blood of many innocent people was shed. However, in its early stages it actually gave Christians hope of opening China to missions and Christian influence. Many Bibles were printed and a great deal of money was given for the cause of Chinese evangelization. Suddenly organizations interested in evangelizing China had plenty of money, but not enough people willing to go and be missionaries. For Hudson Taylor, here at last was the opportunity for which he had been preparing.

Taiping Rebellion

The Taiping Rebellion was a central and important feature dominating the Chinese political scene 1857–64. It was a movement of disappointed peasants who made their capital in Nanking, and from there spread a rebellion to 14 out of 18 provinces of the empire. Apparently, Hung Hsiu-Ch'uan, the founder of the movement, studied Protestant theology. Hong came to believe that he was the Son of God, and the younger brother of Jesus. His mission on earth was to rid China of evil influences. They included Manchus, Taoists, Buddhists, and Confucians. Hong's religion combined traditional Chinese ideas with half-understood Christianity. In 1851, Hong proclaimed a new dynasty, the Taiping, which means 'Great Peace', and assumed the title 'Heavenly King'. Two years later, the Taiping army captured Nanking, a large city in central China. Local warlords led by Tseng Kuo-fan and adventurers from America and Britain combined to surround Nanking in 1862. When they defeated the city two years later, more than 100,000 rebels, including Hong, committed suicide rather than face capture. The Qing Dynasty was so weakened by the rebellion that they lost control of many parts of China to local warlords. Both the Chinese Nationalists and the Communists, two groups that later ruled the nation, claimed to have been inspired by the Taiping Rebellion.

See J.M. Callery and M. Yvan, *History of the Insurrection in China* (London: Smith, Elder & Co., 1853); E.P. Boardman, *Christian Influence upon the Ideology of the Taiping Rebellion, 1851–1864* (Madison: University of Wisconsin Press, 1952); F.H. Michael, *The Taiping Rebellion* (University of Washington Press: Seattle and London, 3 vol., 1966–71).

He had to pass one more test: a test of integrity. At that time there were not many missionary organizations, and most only accepted people who were ordained or educated. Hudson Taylor grappled with the question of whether he should be sent by the CES or go on his own. With them he would have some security and support – but they could also limit his movements while in China, and he wanted to be free to go and do what God told him. They were also paying for his studies, and he had already received some of the money. He knew that before they sent him he needed to be transparent about his struggles regarding this. After much prayer, he wrote a letter to the Society sharing with them why he found it difficult to continue to receive their financial help, and he laid down before them his desire to be free to go when and where God was calling him, rather than being bound by obligations to them.

'Very shortly after this the way cleared suddenly for Hudson Taylor.'[33] Recent developments in China provided an opportunity greater than ever before. Soon, the CES reviewed their requirements, as the door to evangelism in China seemed wide open.

The Taiping Rebellion was on the rise in China. Their aims were to abolish the Manchu dynasty, and cleanse the country of opium and idol worshipers. 'In the early days they [the Taipings] honoured the Bible, attached great importance to the Ten Commandments, used the Lord's Prayer, held daily services at which they sang hymns in honour of the triune God, recited creeds, and listened to sermons. These developments in China naturally aroused intense interest and excitement among Christians in England, Europe and America.'[34] They would all later be bitterly disappointed, but for now everyone believed the path was clear for missionaries.

Hudson Taylor received a letter asking him to consider setting off immediately.

Pray for me, dear Amelia, that He who has promised to meet all our needs may be with me in this painful though long-expected hour. When we look at ourselves – at the littleness of our love, the barrenness of our service, and the small progress we make towards perfection – how soul-refreshing it is to turn and gaze on Him . . . Oh the fullness of Christ: *the fullness of Christ!*[35]

Leaving at last

It was on 19th September 1853 that the *Dumfries* sailed for China; and not until 1st March, in the spring of the following year, did I arrive in Shanghai. Our voyage had a rough beginning, but many had promised to remember us in constant prayer. No small comfort was this; for we had scarcely left the Mersey when a violent equinoctial gale caught us, and for twelve days we were beating backwards and forwards in the Irish Channel, unable to get out to sea. The gale steadily increased, and after almost a week we lay to for a time; but drifting on a lee coast, we were compelled again to make sail, and endeavoured to beat off to windward. The utmost efforts of the captain and crew, however, were unavailing; and Sunday night, 25th September, found us drifting into Carnarvon Bay, each tack becoming shorter, until at last we were within a stone's-throw of the rocks. About this time, as the ship, which had refused to stay, was put round in the other direction, the Christian captain said to me, 'We cannot live half an hour now: what of your call to labour for the Lord in China?' I had previously passed through a time of much conflict, but that was over, and it was a great joy to feel and to tell him that I would not for any consideration be in any other position; that I strongly expected to reach China; but that, if otherwise, at any rate the Master would say it was well that I was found seeking to obey His command! Within a few minutes after wearing ship the captain walked up to the compass, and said to me, 'The wind has freed two points; we shall be able to beat out of the bay.' And so we did. The bowsprit was sprung and the vessel seriously strained; but in a few days we got out to sea, and the necessary repairs were so thoroughly effected on board that our journey to China was in due time satisfactorily accomplished.

One thing was a great trouble to me that night. I was a very young believer, and had not sufficient faith in God to see Him in and through the use of means. I had felt it a duty to comply with the earnest wish of my beloved and honoured mother, and for her sake to procure a swimming-belt. But in my own soul I felt as if I could not simply trust in God while I had this swimming-belt; and my heart had no rest until on that night, after all hope of being saved was gone, I had given it away. Then I had perfect peace; and, strange to say, put several light things together, likely to float at the time we struck, without any thought of inconsistency or scruple. Ever since, I have seen clearly the mistake I made – a mistake that is very common in these days, when erroneous teaching on faith-healing does much harm, misleading some as to the purposes of God, shaking the faith of others, and distressing the minds of many. The use of means ought not to lessen our faith in God; and our faith in God ought not to hinder our using whatever means He has given us for the accomplishment of His own purposes. For years after this I always took a swimming-belt with me, and never had any trouble about it; for after the storm was over, the question was settled for me, through the prayerful study of the Scriptures. God gave me then to see my mistake, probably to deliver me from a great deal of trouble on similar questions now so constantly raised. When in medical or surgical charge of any case, I have never thought of neglecting to ask God's guidance and blessing in the use of appropriate means, nor yet of omitting to give Him thanks for answered prayer and restored health. But to me it would appear as presumptuous and wrong to neglect the use of those measures which He Himself has put within our reach, as to neglect to take daily food, and suppose that life and health might be maintained by prayer alone. The voyage was a very tedious one . . . God encouraged me, ere landing on China's shores, to bring every variety of need to Him in prayer, and to expect that He would honour the Name of the Lord Jesus, and give the help which each emergency required.[36]

This journey can be read as a great metaphor of the ministry of Hudson Taylor . . . sometimes painful and dangerous, sometimes calm and full of goodness and smoother sailing, sometimes so close to the rocks that many thought the end would come soon.

On the voyage they passed by many beautiful islands. Hudson Taylor knew there were people there who needed to hear the gospel also, but he was called to China, and nothing would distract him from it.

A Living Epistle

Key learning points

Spiritual Formation

Become a good steward. Cultivate a spirit of generosity. Give away a growing percentage of your income, and bless others with your possessions.

Trust God. The Bible tells us faith is of greater worth than gold. Hudson Taylor knew that in China he would be utterly dependent on God alone, so he did all he could to stretch and develop his faith before he left.

Recognize God's provision. Don't discard the provision of God through a misunderstanding of faith. Be thankful for all he gives to you.

Relationships are important. They will either make or break your ministry. Although tempted, Hudson Taylor did not compromise in the area of relationships. Marry a partner who won't stand in the way of God's call on your life.

'The way of duty is the way of safety.' Have a sound understanding of spiritual discipline, and keep following even when you do not feel like it. There is a place for performing spiritual acts purely out of duty, since doing so can keep us spiritually alive during our darkest moments.

Leadership Skills

Be transparent about your motives and plans. Make a decision to always be a person of integrity.

Stand on the shoulders of giants. Hudson Taylor was inspired by the life and leadership of George Müller. Find a mentor, read about great women and men of God; learn from them.

Mission Skills

Support local ministry. Hudson Taylor said that going overseas does not make anyone a missionary. Be involved locally before you have an impact globally. Love your local church.

4

Homecoming – First Year in China

1854–55

Following an arduous journey, Hudson Taylor finally arrived at the country he had felt called to for years. But his difficulties as a missionary were only just beginning. There were still many preparations he needed to undertake before he could begin sharing the gospel amongst the Chinese.

Arrival in China

The wind ceased, the rain stopped, and the tired sails were folded to rest. There he stood, a lonely, cold and tiny figure, his head still spinning after a dangerous six-month sea journey. He had come to a place he did not know: a place he already loved and had been consumed with for years, though he had never placed so much as one foot on its soil.

China did not welcome him warmly. There was misery, decay and death all around him, both spiritual and physical.

We get used to comforts very easily and quickly. Many of us cannot imagine life without a computer or mobile phone any more. In the nineteenth century there were no simple ways of finding out about a different country; no way to log online and check the climate, the best hotels, and the history and culture of a place. The world has grown smaller today with modern transport and communications. At that time, it took several months to receive a letter.

Let us just stop here for a moment and take it all in. Imagine that day, Wednesday 1 March 1854. Imagine the scene . . . one man at the edge of the sea of humanity. There they stood – the unreached (as we now call them), the unevangelized. There he stood, maybe only now realizing that he was so very far away from home. There stood the drug addicts and the victims of war, the wretched and the poorest of the poor. There he stood, at first seeing only men as trees walking.

Poor, yet rich in God, weak, yet strong in the power of the Holy Spirit, he looked into the streets stretching before him. As the fog started to lift, Hudson Taylor began to see the contours of the buildings and people.

My feelings on stepping ashore, I cannot attempt to describe. My heart felt as though it had not room and must burst its bonds, while tears of gratitude and thankfulness fell from my eyes.

Mingled with thankfulness for the deliverance from many dangers and joy at finding myself at last on Chinese soil came a vivid realisation of the great distance between me and those I loved, and that I was a stranger in a strange land.[37]

China was in the middle of a brutal war. The Taiping rebels were making their progress towards Beijing. The continuous fighting contributed to a growing famine, which in turn caused rising food prices. Finding a place to live was also difficult.

On landing in Shanghai on 1st March 1854, I found myself surrounded with difficulties that were wholly unexpected. A band of rebels, known as the 'Red Turbans,' had taken possession of the native city, against which was encamped an Imperial army of from forty to fifty thousand men, who were a much greater source of discomfort and danger to the little European community than were the rebels themselves. Upon landing, I was told that to live outside the Settlement was impossible, while within the foreign concession apartments were scarcely obtainable at any price. The dollar, now worth about three shillings, had risen to a value of eight and ninepence, and the prospect for one with only a small income of English money was dark indeed. However, I had three letters of introduction, and counted on counsel and help, especially from one of those to whom I had been commended, whose friends I well knew and highly valued. Of course I sought him out at once, but only to learn that he had been buried a month or two before, having died from fever during the time of my voyage.

Saddened by these tidings, I inquired for a missionary to whom another of my letters of introduction was addressed; but a further disappointment awaited me – he had left for America. The third letter remained; but as it had been given by a comparative stranger, I had expected less from it than from the other two. It proved, however, to be God's channel of help. The Rev. Dr. Medhurst, of the London Mission, to whom it was addressed, introduced me to Dr. Lockhart, who kindly allowed me to live with him for six months. Dr. Medhurst procured my first Chinese teacher; and he, Dr. Edkins, and the late Mr. Alexander Wylie gave me considerable help with the language.[38]

Drs Lockhard and Medhurst were leading missionaries at that time. Medhurst was the author of the first book on China Hudson Taylor had ever read. Soon, he was assisting Medhurst in the hospital, and Medhurst advised him to learn Mandarin (he and his cousin had been attempting to teach themselves the Hong Kong dialect of Cantonese back in England). At first he struggled with the language, and became frustrated with his lack of ability to communicate with people. All this was made worse by his housing problems.

The cold was so great and other things so trying; that I scarcely knew what I was doing or saying at first. Then, what it means to be so far away from home, at the seat of war, and not able to understand or be understood by the people was fully realised. Their utter wretchedness and misery, and my inability to help them or even to point them to Jesus, powerfully affected me.[39]

On Saturday (March 4th) I took a walk through the market and such a muddy, dirty place as Shanghai I never did see! The ground is all mud; dry in dry weather, but an hour's rain makes it like walking through a clay-field. It scarcely is walking, but wading! I found that there was no probability of getting a house or even apartments, and felt cast down in spirit.[40]

A lonely calling

The city was a place of burned-down houses, poverty, fear, constant violence and death. All the preparations of the previous years were not sufficient in the face of all he encountered. The pressing need to understand and be understood was growing upon him, and drove him to devote every free minute to study. On top of all this distress and heartache he felt lonely. He wrote in a letter:

I would give anything for a friend with whom to consult freely. My position is so perplexing that if I had not definite promises of Divine guidance to count on, I do not know what I should do. There is, I fear, no probability of my being able to keep within my salary under present circumstances. If I had quarters of my own I could live on rice (not bread, that would be too expensive) and drink tea without milk or sugar, which is cheaper enough here. But that I cannot do now. Things are increasing in expense all the while and dollars are getting dear.[41]

He felt isolated from the missionary circle there and worried he was a burden to them. He wasn't one of them after all. He had been sent in a hurry, with unrealistic and misled expectations, by an organization that was laughed at by missionaries in Shanghai. Most of the missionaries at that time were well educated and usually amply resourced: plus they received high fees from the government for helping with translations. They did well, and confined themselves to the safety of the five treaty ports of Canton, Amoy, Foochow, Ningpo and Shanghai.

Opium Wars (1839-42 and 1856-60)

Even though Chinese law prohibited the trade of opium, tonnes of this product were imported by British merchants from India. The addiction was growing in China and many made huge profits on it. In 1839, the Chinese attacked the ships carrying the opium and destroyed all the cargo. Britain fought back and defeated them, forcing them to sign the Treaty of Nanking: as a result Hong Kong was ceded to England, and five main ports were opened to trade: Canton, Amoy, Foochow, Ningpo and Shang-hai. The unequal treaty was humiliating to China.

Hudson Taylor was, therefore, very much on his own. The CES did not understand the economic situation and the rising food prices, even though he explained to them in letters many times that the money they allocated for him was nowhere near enough. He lived on hopelessly small amounts. The CES not only was incompetent at keeping in touch with Hudson Taylor and providing for him, but they also burdened him with unreasonable demands; for example, to find accommodation for Dr Parker's family who were on their way to China. He was distressed in his soul, tired and ill in his body, with deteriorating eyesight due to the darkness in which he had to read and study. It was not an inspiring beginning to a lifelong mission. Yet, through it all, he found ways to keep himself occupied and even entertained.

April 25: Ordered a cabinet for insects, and worked at Chinese and photography.

April 28: Very warm again. Worked at Chinese five hours. Had a bad headache all day. Caught a few insects as a commencement of my collection.

April 29: At Chinese six hours. After dinner took a walk in search of nocturnal insects. Had some dfficulty in getting into the Settlement again, the gates being closed.[42]

And another record of his busy days

Before breakfast read Medicine, then Chinese nearly seven hours. After dinner, Greek and Latin exercises, each an hour. After pouring over these things till one can scarcely see, it is a comfort to have a fine, clear, large type Bible, such as Aunt Hardey gave me. It is quite a luxury. Well, all these studies are necessary. Some of them, the classical languages of Europe, ought to have been mastered long ago, so it is now or never with me. But the sweetest duties of the day are those that lead to Jesus – prayer, reading and meditation upon His precious Word.[43]

Accommodation problems

His life was not easy. He still did not have permanent housing, and now he was asked by the Society to provide accommodation for a family that was on their way to join him. No, this was not a mistake – they were definitely coming! How could he possibly find accommodation for a whole family when he hadn't even been able to find a room for himself? This caused him more distress, and he became an object of gossip among fellow missionaries: they knew the Parker family had set out, getting closer each day, and suspected Hudson Taylor was not doing enough to find and furnish rooms for them. Only God's amazing intervention could lead him to a place; the rooms he eventually found were not wonderful, but they were all there was.

After six months' stay with Dr. Lockhart, I rented a native house outside the Settlement, and commenced a little missionary work amongst my Chinese neighbours, which for a few months continued practicable. When the French joined the Imperialists in attacking the city, the position of my house became so dangerous that during the last few weeks, in consequence of nightly recurring skirmishes, I gave up attempting to sleep except in the daytime. One night a fire appeared very near, and I climbed up to a little observatory I had arranged on the roof of the house, to see whether it was necessary to attempt escape. While there a ball struck the ridge of the roof on the opposite side of the quadrangle, showering pieces of broken tile all around me, while the ball itself rolled down into the court below. It weighed four or five pounds; and had it come a few inches higher, would probably have spent its force on me instead of on the building. My dear mother kept the ball for many years. Shortly after this I had to abandon the house and return to the Foreign Settlement – a step that was taken none too soon, for before the last of my belongings were removed, the house was burnt to the ground.[44]

The longest valley

At this time he drew much encouragement from the commentary on Psalm 84 by C.H. Rappard-Gobat, once a missionary himself.

Speaking to my students one day . . . I asked them 'Young men, which is the longest, widest, most populous valley in the world?' And they began to summon up all their geographical information to answer me. But it was not the valley of the Yangtze, the Congo, or the Mississippi. Nay, this Jammerthal, as it is in our German, this valley of Baca, or Weeping, exceeds them all. For six thousand years we trace it back, filled all the way with an innumerable multitude. For every life passes at some time into the Valley of Weeping. But the point for us is not what do we suffer here, but what do we leave behind us? What have we made of it, this long, dark Valley, for ourselves and others? What is our attitude, as we pass through its shadows? Do we desire only, chiefly, the shortest way out? Or do we seek to find it, to make it, according to His Promise, 'a place of springs': here a spring and there a spring, for the blessing of others and the glory of Our God? Thus it is with the man 'whose strength is in Thee.' He has learned the preciousness of this Jammerthal, and that these dry, hard places yield the springs for which hearts are thirsting the wide world over. So St. Paul in his life. What a long journey he had to make through the Valley of Weeping! 'In labours more abundant, in stripes above measure, in prisons more frequent, in deaths oft. Of the Jews five times received I forty stripes save one. Thrice was I beaten with rods, once was I stoned, thrice I suffered shipwreck, a night and a day have I been in the deep' . . . A long journey indeed through the Valley of Weeping; but oh, what springs of blessing! What rain filling the pools! We drink of it still today.[45]

In one of his many letters to his sister he wrote:

What a very different thing it is to review the aggregate success of Missions and missionaries over many years from taking part in the process itself with all its trials and discouragements. But let us be comforted. So will it be for us too at last. One smile from Him we love will repay all the sorrows, and leave a clear balance to the good of whatever has been accomplished.

Oh Amelia, one needs an anchor for one's faith . . . and thank God we have it! The promises of God stand sure. 'The Lord knoweth them that are His.' How easy it is to talk about economy, the high salaries of missionaries, and all the rest. But there is more than one missionary here who hardly knows how to manage to make both ends meet. Well, if we want a city, there is one we can turn back to. But no, we will be pilgrims and strangers here, looking for a better home, 'that is an heavenly', 'whose builder and maker is God.' Oh that those around us had the same hope!

You ask how I get over my troubles. This is the way . . . I take them to the Lord. Since writing the above, I have been reading my evening portion. The Old Testament part of it happens to be the 72nd to the 74th Psalms. Read them as I have if you want to see how applicable they are. I don't know how it is, but I seldom can read Scripture now without tears of joy and gratitude.

I see that to be as I am and have been since my arrival has really been more conducive to improvement and progress than any other position would have been, though in many respects it has been painful and far from what I should have chosen for myself. Oh for more implicit reliance on the wisdom and love of God![46]

He described his house to a friend:

The Chinese house to which I am removing is in a dangerous position, being beyond the protection of the Settlement and liable to injury from both Imperialists and Rebels. The former have threatened to burn the street, and the latter have two cannons constantly pointing at it. My teacher who comes from a distance dare not go there, and as I cannot get another who speaks Mandarin at present I shall have to commence the study of the Shanghai dialect . . . As I can talk with my present teacher tolerably well, it is a trial to lose him and commence again from the beginning. But as there is no hope of being able to go to Mandarin-speaking districts for several years, and the Shanghai dialect I can use as I learn it, this too no doubt is wisely ordered. At any rate I am thankful that my way is hedged up on every side, so that no choice is left me. I am obliged to go forward . . . And if you hear of my being killed or injured, do not think it a pity that I came, but thank God I was permitted to distribute some Scriptures and tracts and to speak a few words in broken Chinese for Him who died for me.[47]

September was a difficult, anxious month for him.

> Though in some ways I never passed a more anxious month in my life, I have never felt before so conscious of God's presence with me. I begin to enjoy the sweet, peaceful rest in the Lord and in His promises experienced first in Hull. That was the brightest part of my spiritual life, and how poor at the best! Since then I have been in a declining state, but the Lord has brought me back, and as there is no standing still in these things, I trust to go on to apprehend heights and depths, lengths and breadths of love divine far exceeding anything I have yet entered into. May God grant it, for Jesus' sake.[48]

His biographers, Dr and Mrs Howard Taylor, wrote:

> One cannot but be impressed in reading the letters of this period with the sacred ambition of Hudson Taylor's prayers; a subject worth pondering, if it be true that prayer moulds the life and not circumstances, and that as are our deepest desires before God so will the trend of our outward experiences be. Certainly nothing is more significant in the life before us than the longing for usefulness and likeness to the Lord he loved. Not honour or success, but usefulness, 'widespread usefulness,' was his constant prayer. Would he have drawn back could he have foreseen that the only way to its fulfilment was through the furnace seven times heated? For much preparatory work had yet to be done. His prayers were indeed to be answered

beyond anything he asked or thought; but he must pray with yet fuller meaning, and go through with all the training needed at the Master's hands. The iron must be tempered to steel, and his heart made stronger and more tender than others, through having loved and suffered more, with God. He was pioneering a way in China, little as he or anyone else could imagine it, for hundreds who were to follow. Every burden must be his, every trial known as only experience can teach it. He who was to be used of God to dry so many tears, must himself weep. He who was to encourage thousands in a life of child-like trust, must learn in his own case deep lessons of a Father's loving care. So difficulties were permitted to gather about him, especially at first when every impression was vivid and lasting, difficulties attended by many a deliverance to cheer him on his way.

As much of his usefulness later on was to consist in helping and providing for young missionaries, it is not to be wondered at that a large part of his preparation at this time had to do with financial matters and the unintentional mismanagement of the home Committee. He had to learn how to do and how not to do for those who on the human side would be dependent on him; a lesson of vital importance, lying at the very foundation of his future work. Hence all this trial about a small, settled income and large uncertain needs; about irregularity of mails and long-unanswered letters; about rapidly-changing opportunities of service on the field, and the slow-moving ideas and inaccessibility of Committees at home. He did his best, and the inexperienced Secretaries in London did their best also, as faithful men of God. But something, somehow, was wanting; and just what it was Hudson

Taylor had to discover, and later on to remedy. Seen in this light it need hardly be said a special significance attaches to his financial cares; and the letters in which he tells at times so touchingly of the exercise of mind through which he was passing have an interest all of their own. The iron – one sees it – was entering into his very soul; but from this long endurance was to spring heart's-ease for many another.[49]

In autumn 1854 Dr Parker and his family finally arrived, to the basic but precious accommodation Hudson Taylor had been able to secure. Dr Parker soon learned the Society did not supply them with enough resources in the face of growing inflation, and, together with Hudson Taylor, made many appeals for help. The winter was coming soon.

No one who has not experienced it can understand the effect of such incessant strain in mind and body. It makes one so nervous and irritable that we sorely need your prayers as well as our own to enable us at all times to manifest a proper spirit.

How gracious of God thus to keep us from being deluded into supposing that we are free from the evils that belong to fallen nature, and to make us long the more earnestly for the time when we shall see our blessed Master and be perfected in His likeness. Thank the Lord, there does remain a rest for us. I am so apt to grow weary and selfishly wish I were there, instead of desiring only to do His will and wait His time; to follow the footsteps of Jesus and finish all that He will give me to do. Indeed, the work of grace seems only just begun in my heart. I have been an unfruitful branch, and need no small amount of pruning. May the present trials result only in blessing, preparing me for more extensive usefulness here and a crown of rejoicing hereafter. The continued strain, to which I have been subjected of late, has caused a degree of nervous irritability never before experienced, requiring the greatest watchfulness to prevent the manifestation of an unsuitable spirit before those by whom I am surrounded. What a solemn thing it is to be a witness for God, sent into the midst of heathen darkness to show forth in our lives all that by our words we teach . . . pray for me that I may have more grace, humility and reliance on the power of God, that I may prove henceforth more efficient, by His blessing, in this holy service.[50]

The first year of his ministry in China was drawing to an end, and it had not been an easy year by any means: full of the dangers of war, poverty, lack of companionship and, in fact, lack of everything. However, though the political situation was difficult Hudson Taylor and Dr Parker were able to visit a few villages outside the Settlement. Shortly afterwards, he was able to set out on his first evangelistic journey.

The great enemy is always ready with his oft-repeated suggestion, 'All these things are against me.' But oh, how false the word! The cold, and even the hunger, the watchings and sleeplessness of nights of danger, and the feeling at times of utter isolation and helplessness, were well and wisely chosen, and tenderly and lovingly meted out. What circumstances could have rendered the Word of God more sweet, the presence of God more real, the help of God more precious? These were times, indeed, of emptying and humbling, but were experiences that made not ashamed, and that strengthened purpose to go forward as God might direct, with His *proved* promise, 'I will not fail thee, nor forsake thee.' One can see, even now, that 'as for God, His way is perfect,' and yet can rejoice that the missionary path of today is comparatively a smooth and an easy one.

Journeying inland was contrary to treaty arrangements and attended with much difficulty, especially for some time after the battle of Muddy Flat, in which an Anglo-American contingent of about three hundred marines and seamen, with a volunteer corps of less than a hundred residents, attacked the Imperial camp, and drove away from thirty to fifty thousand Chinese soldiers, the range of our shot and shell making the native artillery useless.[51]

Homecoming – First Year in China

Key learning points

Spiritual Formation

Suffering can destroy us, or make us stronger. Suffering and distress was a part of Hudson Taylor's preparation. Later on he would be able to empathize with people more because of the experiences he had endured.

Leadership Skills

Learn to be flexible. There will often be unexpected situations. Learn to deal with them with wisdom and patience.

Sometimes leadership is a lonely position. Wherever you can, work in a team rather than on your own. Don't neglect your friends, as you will need them during the lonely times.

Develop a hobby. Have something you do which is not a part of your ministry. It will work wonders for your mental health, especially during periods of stress and anxiety.

5

The Sound of Many Rivers

1855–60

With the mission work finally underway, the next six years would be a great beginning to a new work of God in China. Many came to faith, the vision started to become reality, and Hudson Taylor found a long-awaited companion for his life and ministry.

Fruitful journeys

Hudson Taylor set off on his first missionary journey on 16 December 1854. Travelling on a Chinese houseboat he and his companion, Dr. Edkins, gave out tracts and preached among the people, generating interest even among the Buddhist monks. During this journey, and others that followed, Hudson Taylor got to know more and more of the culture and customs of the Chinese people he loved so much. Some of the trips brought much fruit, while some brought dangers, but all reinforced his realization of how much there was to be done.

Even though the times were difficult, Hudson Taylor was able to make eight trips into the interior, and learnt a great deal from each one. Not only did he see the

Shanghai is now in peace, but it is the peace of death. 2,000 people at the very least have perished, and the tortures some of the victims have undergone cannot have been exceeded by the worst barbarities of the Inquisition. The city is little more than a mass of ruins, and many of the wretched objects who have survived are piteous to behold.

How dreadful is the war! From the South to the North Gate of Shanghai, on one side only, sixty-six heads and several bodies are exposed by the sanguinary Imperialists, including those of old men with white hair, women and children . . . These terrible sights are now so common that they do not upset as they did at first. But it is impossible to witness them without feelings of intense abhorrence for the Government that permits and even perpetrates such atrocities.

After the retaking of Shanghai by the Imperialists, in February 1855, I was enabled to rent a house within the walls of the native city, and gladly availed myself of this opportunity to reside amidst the crowded population left to inhabit the ruins that had survived the war. Here I made my headquarters, though often absent on more or less prolonged itinerations.[53]

multitudes he had come to evangelize and the conditions in which they lived, he also saw something of the results of his work and plenty of interest in the message of the gospel. He decided he needed to grow in Christ and continue to feed upon the Word of God if he were to remain useful, and to persevere with such a demanding ministry. 'What I need is more faith, more intimate communion with God . . . We can impart that only which we first receive.'[54]

In autumn 1855 he met William Burns, who became a close friend and companion in his missionary journeys. The relationship was a source of great encouragement to them both. Burns spirituality challenged and inspired Hudson Taylor; he was full of stories and testimonies about revivals in different parts of the world, he was passionate about the Word of God, and discerning when it came to the aspects of mission.

Those happy months were an unspeakable joy and privilege to me. His love for the Word was delightful, and his holy, reverential life and constant communings with God made fellowship with him satisfying to the deep cravings of my heart. His accounts of revival work and of persecutions in Canada, and Dublin, and in Southern China were most instructive, as well as interesting; for with true spiritual insight he often pointed out God's purposes in trial in a way that made all life assume quite a new aspect and value. His views especially about evangelism as the great work of the Church, and the order of lay evangelists as a lost order that Scripture required to be restored, were seed-thoughts which were to prove fruitful in the subsequent organisation of the China Inland Mission.[55]

A change of clothes

Hudson Taylor in turn proved to Burns that wearing traditional Chinese clothes opened doors, and set people at ease in a way an English outfit never would. Most foreign missionaries considered wearing Chinese dress a humiliation, but Hudson Taylor realized English clothes were a distraction to the Chinese, who became fascinated by them rather than the missionary's message.

> We journeyed together, evangelising cities and towns in southern Kiang-Su and north Cheh-kiang, living in our boats, and following the course of the canals and rivers which here spread like a network over the whole face of the rich and fertile country. Mr. Burns at that time was wearing English dress; but saw that while I was the younger and in every way less experienced, I had the quiet hearers, while he was followed by the rude boys, and by the curious but careless; that I was invited to the homes of the people, while he received an apology that the crowd that would follow precluded his being invited. After some weeks of observation he also adopted the native dress, and enjoyed the increased facilities which it gave.[56]

Adopting Chinese dress was an extremely important strategic move on behalf of Hudson Taylor. It brought disdain upon him from fellow missionaries in Shanghai but he was amazed how many doors opened to the gospel through wearing it. Even his family could not fully understand why he did it. In a letter to his sister he explained:

> I am sorry that the change is disagreeable to you, but you will regret it very little when you learn that without it we could never gain a footing in this important place . . . A little thought will, I am sure, enable you to realise that if the Chinese costume seems so barbarous to us, our English

dress must be no less to them, and that it cannot but be a hindrance in going amongst them in the friendly ways necessary to securing their confidence and affection . . . without it we could not stay here a single day. That Miss – does not like it I am very sorry to hear, but that does not make me regret that I have adopted it. It is one of those matters about which I and my beloved companion, Mr. Burns, thank God almost every day.[57]

Opium slaves

About two hundred boxes of opium are imported monthly; each box contains forty balls of about four pounds in weight. Thus not less than thirty-two thousand pounds weight of opium enter China every month at this port alone, the cost of which is about a quarter of a million sterling. After this you will not be surprised to learn that the people are wretchedly poor, ignorant, and vicious. A cruel slave trade also is carried on under the name of the 'coolie traffic.' The men are engaged (nominally) for a certain term of years, but few live to return. A bounty is paid them, and they are told that they are going to make their fortunes, or they are entrapped by worse means. Once on the ship the agent receives so much a head for the poor fellows who soon find themselves in captivity of the most horrible kind. Some jump overboard in their efforts to escape, but they are generally retaken and flogged. Some ships carry a thousand and others three or four hundred, and very many die before reaching their destination – Cuba, Havanna and Callao . . . Of one ship with several hundreds on board, I heard the surgeon say that not more than two-thirds would survive the voyage. Poor people! One only is able to help them. Oh, for His blessing![58]

Opium Wars

The British and French again defeated China in a second opium war in 1856. By the terms of the Treaty of Tientsin (1858) the Chinese opened new ports to trading and allowed foreigners to travel in the interior. Christians gained the right to spread their faith and hold property, thus opening up another means of western penetration. The United States and Russia gained the same privileges in separate treaties. But these unequal treaties left the Chinese feeling disgraced and, later on, contributed to the rise of the Boxer Rebellion (1900).

'Opium entered China on the back of the camel and ended up breaking the back of the whole nation' (*The Opium Wars: The Addiction of One Empire and the Corruption of Another*, W. Trafis Hanes, p. xii).

As foreigners it is no surprise they were often mistreated. As Hudson Taylor himself said, they would have been close to death on many occasions if it were not for direct intervention from God. It is truly amazing that in an atmosphere so hostile they were able to do so much.

Fire and theft

He was forced to return to Shanghai to replace his medicine stock. On arrival he found that the premises of the

If ever there were a place needing the blessing of the Gospel, it is certainly this place. Men are sunk so low in sin as to have lost all sense of shame . . . lower even than the beasts that perish. The official classes are as bad as the rest and instead of restraining evil are governed themselves by opium and love of money. Sin does indeed reign here, and, as always, those most to be pitied and whose case seems most hopeless are the women.[59]

London mission, where he kept his much needed outfits and medicine, had been destroyed by fire. This caused him a great deal of grief, discouragement and confusion. Medicines were far too expensive to buy in Shanghai, but he could not do without them. He decided to make his way to Ningpo, hoping Dr Parker (who was based there now) might have some additional supplies.

On his way to Ningpo the person carrying his luggage disappeared, taking with him all his belongings. Hudson Taylor was forced to sleep outside on many occasions, sometimes at the steps of a Buddhist temple. Even though he had a right to complain about the theft and demand compensation and the punishment of the thief he never reported the incident. Because of the way he dealt with the robbery he gained a lifelong friend – George Müller. He somehow heard of what had happened and was touched by Hudson Taylor's response to it. He sent money in order to cover the missing goods, and became the most faithful supporter of the ministry of Hudson Taylor for many years to come.

In Ningpo Hudson Taylor met Maria Dyer, an orphaned daughter of missionary parents, who spoke fluent Ningpo dialect and was involved in ministry in a school there together with her sister. After obtaining medicines from Dr Parker, Hudson Taylor set off to be reunited with William Burns. However, things had changed: a letter from Burns told him that after a recent arrest and six-week imprisonment he had moved to Guangzhou. Hudson Taylor, therefore, returned to Ningpo, more than happy to see Maria again.

As winter drew on I rented a native house in Wu-gyiao-deo, or Lake Head Street. It was not then a very comfortable residence. I have a very distinct remembrance of tracing my initials on the snow which during the night had collected upon my coverlet in the large barn-like upper room, now subdivided into four or five smaller ones, each of which is comfortably ceiled. The tiling of an unceiled Chinese house may keep off the rain – if it happens to be sound – but it does not afford so good a protection against snow, which will beat up through crannies and crevices, and find its way within. But however unfinished may have been its fittings, the little house was well adapted for work amongst the people; and there I thankfully settled down, finding ample scope for service, – morning, noon, and night.[60]

Leaving the Chinese Evangelisation Society

At this point Hudson Taylor stopped drawing money from the CES, revealing an important aspect of his character.

Personally, I had always avoided debt, and kept within my salary, though at times only by very careful economy. Now there was no difficulty in doing this, for my income was larger, and the country being in a more peaceful state, things were not so dear. But the Society itself was in debt. The quarterly bills which I and others were instructed to draw were often met with borrowed money, and a correspondence commenced which terminated in the following year by my resigning from conscientious motives.

To me it seemed that the teaching of God's Word was unmistakably clear: 'Owe no man anything.' To borrow money implied, to my mind, a contradiction of Scripture – a confession that God had withheld some good thing, and a determination to get for ourselves what He had not given. Could that which was wrong for one Christian to do be right for an association of Christians? Or could any amount of precedents make a wrong course justifiable? If the Word taught me anything, it taught me to have no connection with debt. I could not think that God was poor, that He was short of resources, or unwilling to supply any want of whatever work was really His. It seemed to me that if there were lack of funds to carry on work, then to that degree, in that special development, or at that time, it could not be the work of God. To satisfy my conscience I was therefore compelled to resign my connection with the Society.

It was a great satisfaction to me that my friend and colleague, Mr. Jones . . . was led to take the same step, and we were both profoundly thankful that the separation took place without the least breach of friendly feeling on either side. Indeed, we had the joy of knowing that the step we took commended itself to several members of the

Committee, although the Society as a whole could not come to our position. Depending on God alone for supplies, we were enabled to continue a measure of connection with our former supporters, sending home journals, etc., for publication as before, so long as the Society continued to exist.

The step we had taken was not a little trying to faith. I was not at all sure what God would have me do, or whether He would so meet my need as to enable me to continue working as before . . . I was willing to give up all my time to the service of evangelisation among the heathen if, by any means, He would supply the smallest amount on which I could live; and if He were not pleased to do this, I was prepared to undertake whatever work might be necessary to support myself, giving all the time that could be spared from such a calling to more distinctly missionary efforts.

But God blessed and prospered me, and how glad and thankful I felt when the separation was really effected! I could look right up into my Father's face with a satisfied heart, ready by His grace to do the next thing as He might teach me, and feeling very sure of His loving care.

And how blessedly He did lead me I can never, never tell. It was like a continuation of some of my earlier experiences at home. My faith was not untried; it often, often failed, and I was so sorry and ashamed of the failure to trust such a Father. But oh! I was learning to know Him. I would not even then have missed the trial. He became so near, so real, so intimate. The occasional difficulty about funds never came from an insufficient supply for personal needs, but in consequence of ministering to the wants of scores of the hungry and dying around us.[61]

Even though God guided him in the decision to leave the CES because of their debt, it was not an easy thing to do. He was almost penniless.

> Many seem to think that I am very poor. This certainly is true enough in one sense, but I thank God it is 'as poor, yet making many rich; as having nothing, yet possessing all things.' And my God shall supply *all* my need; to Him be all the glory. I would not, if I could, be otherwise than I am – entirely dependent myself upon the Lord, and used as a channel of help to others.[62]

Falling in love

Nevertheless, God was working on his behalf, and he was answering the prayer for a companion. All these years of believing God does not withhold any good thing were all worth it: Hudson Taylor was falling in love with Maria Dyer. Maria returned his feelings, but Mrs Aldersey, who was looking after Maria and her sister, did not agree to their engagement, thinking very little of Hudson Taylor, 'called by no one, connected to no one, and recognized by no one as a minister of the Gospel.'[63] Yet God's will prevailed. The couple obtained a letter from Maria's guardians in England and were able to marry. The whole process took months of prayer and waiting upon God. The ceremony took place on 20 January 1858. The marriage was a source of much strength, and made the missionary work even more effective.

Hers had been a life connection with missionary work in that great empire; for her father, the loved and devoted Samuel Dyer, was amongst the very earliest representatives of the London Mission in the East. He reached the Straits as early as 1827, and for sixteen years laboured assiduously amongst the Chinese in Penang and Singapore, completing at the same time a valuable fount of Chinese metallic type, the first of the kind that had then been attempted. Dying in 1843, it was never Mr. Dyer's privilege to realise his hopes of ultimately being able to settle on Chinese soil; but his children lived to see the country opened to the Gospel, and to take their share in the great work that had been so dear to his heart. At the time of her marriage, my dear wife had been already living for several years in Ningpo with her friend, Mrs Aldersey, in whose varied missionary operations she was well qualified to render valuable assistance.

After a brief honeymoon, on which they both caught typhoid, they settled in modest attic accommodation in Ningpo, and straightaway resumed the missionary work, investing all their time in young converts and raising up leaders. This period was marked with some amazing provisions and conversions.

The setting was not auspicious: the Taiping rebels

were still around and the Second Opium War was in full swing.

'We feel that we are living only from night to day and day to night,' wrote one of the missionaries, who remained in the city.

The people are thirsting for revenge . . . they mix up together missionaries, traders and the government, the warm and the coolie traffic . . . and say that the kidnapped Chinese are put in the front of the fight against their own Emperor . . . they have placarded the streets calling for our blood; one of the foremost in all this being a man who supplies the Mandarins with buckets to contain the heads of the decapitated, a fearful large trade here.[65]

After the sudden death of his wife, Mr Parker decided to take his four little children back to Scotland. Hudson Taylor and Maria (who had only recently narrowly escaped death due to her own illness) took over the work of the hospital in Ningpo.

Calling for more missionaries

Hudson Taylor's health was not good either. The six years of hard work in China, in hard conditions, had taken its toll on him, and, in March 1859, he suspected he was having trouble with tuberculosis and decided to return to Britain. Because of his experience working and ministering in the hospital in Ningpo he also realized that in order to continue the work he needed more workers. They left for England in 1860 together with their daughter Grace and the Chinese painter Wang-Lae-djün. (Grace had been born in July 1859; they would also have three sons over the next few years.) Before they did so he wrote to his mother:

> Do you know any earnest, devoted young men desirous of serving God in China, who not wanting for more than their actual support would be willing to come out and labour here? Oh, for four or five such helpers! They would probably begin to preach in Chinese in six months' time; and in answer to prayer the necessary means would be found to their support.[66]

Meanwhile, a Great Revival was happening in Britain. God was at work, and Hudson Taylor was soon to tap into its great resources.

'What I desire to know is how I may best serve China; if I am too ill to labour and by returning home might re-establish health, if only for a time, or if I might rouse others to take up the work I can no longer continue, I think I ought to try'.[67]

The Sound of Many Rivers

Key learning points

Spiritual Formation

Continue to grow in Christ. Do not plateau in your spiritual formation. Hudson Taylor knew in order to meet the demands of his ministry he had to keep on maturing in Christ. He constantly expected God to speak through His Word, and to bring answers to prayers.

Avoid debt. Hudson Taylor had strong principles regarding money. He believed debt was contrary to God's will, claiming, 'God's work done, in God's way, will never lack God's resources.'

Discerning Vision

Recognize God can guide through opportunities. The theft of his own belongings and the arrest of Burns could have been severe setbacks to the outreach, but Hudson Taylor discerned through it all the hand of God guiding him to settle in Ningpo.

Don't wait for everything to be right. Do the little you can now. Be courageous, and don't be afraid to leave the safety of the 'treaty ports'.

Mission Skills

Identify with those you want to reach. Hudson Taylor adopted Chinese dress, a radical move at that time. He stood by his decision even though people laughed and mocked him for it.

Invest your time in people. Look after new converts. See them flourish. Hudson Taylor spent a lot of time mentoring and discipling young people, and raising up leaders.

6

Enlarge the Place of Your Tent

1860–66

The enforced return to England could not deter Hudson Taylor's determination and heart for China. Even during convalescence, all his time and attention were devoted to furthering the mission. The years of absence only served to strengthen his resolve, and enabled him to form the China Inland Mission: this would profoundly strengthen the work in China.

'Much of the world's work is done by pent-up forces. The steam which drives the engine does so because it is conserved and fettered. Its limitations are the secret of its power. And this is sometimes true in human life. What are the yearnings of the heart but the pent-up forces of love? And nothing can so intensify these as to hedge in their activities.'[68]

Returning to London

After coming back, Hudson Taylor was told by his doctor he would probably not be able to return to China. As we know, he had never been strong, but after strenuous years in the mission field, working hard in the heat of summer and the cold of severe winter, he was not in good health at all.

He and Maria settled in east London, where he started to complete his medical studies and, together with his Chinese helper and Revd F.F. Gough from the Missionary Society, commenced the translation of the New Testament into the Ningpo dialect. He always returned to his vision for the evangelization of the Chinese inland provinces. He could not forget the millions there. His perseverance was remarkable. He never gave up; never wasted a moment. With a map of China on the wall of his small room he waited and prayed, and felt as close to the people he loved as if they were right there with him.

As a long absence from China appeared inevitable, the next question was how best to serve China while in England, and this led to my engaging for several years, with the late Rev. F. F. Gough of the C. M. S., in the revision of a version of the New Testament in the colloquial of Ningpo for the British and Foreign Bible Society. In undertaking this work, in my short-sightedness I saw nothing beyond the use that the Book, and the marginal references, would be to the native Christians; but I have often seen since that, without those months of feeding and feasting on the Word of God, I should have been quite unprepared to form, on its present basis, a mission like the China Inland Mission.[69]

Soon they were able to see off five missionaries.

The first, Mr. Meadows, sailed for China with his young wife in January 1862, through the kind co-operation and aid of our friend Mr. Berger. The second left England in 1864, having her passage provided by the Foreign Evangelisation Society. The third and fourth reached Ningpo on July 24th, 1865. A fifth soon followed them, reaching Ningpo in September 1865. Thus the prayer for the five workers was fully answered; and we were encouraged to look to God for still greater things.[70]

When Hudson Taylor was forced to take a step back, God, who works in everything for good, helped him to see the needs of inland China even more clearly. While on the mission field he always had to deal with the most immediate needs, and he could only see one move at a time, only a town or a village at a time. Now, as he looked at the huge interior of China on his wall map, he pondered for many hours over the massive need there still was, and he started to strategize about the best way in which to go about this task. In the past he had been disappointed with the missionary society that sent him: therefore, he wanted to make sure he would take much better care of the workers he supported in the field. A great deal of time was thus spent in correspondence and prayer for them.

Feasting on the Word

The work carried out from his tiny room bore fruit in the spiritual dimension also. By studying the Word of God carefully in order to ensure a good translation, Hudson Taylor was himself fed by it.

In the study of the Divine Word I learned that to obtain successful labourers, not elaborate appeals for help, but first, earnest prayer to God to thrust labourer, and second the deepening of the spiritual life of the church, so that men should be unable to stay at home, were what was needed. I saw that Apostolic plan was not to raise ways and means, but to go and to do the work, trusting in the sure word, which had said, 'Seek first the Kingdom of God and His righteousness, and all these things shall be added to you.'[71]

Marshall Broomhall writes:

At the same time as this wider vision of China's need was being given, a deeper insight into God's purposes was being gained. The message to Israel of old was coming home to him – 'Enlarge the place of thy tent, and let them stretch forth the curtains of thine habitations; spare not, lengthen thy cords and strengthen thy stakes.' The daily sight of that map of China, with its vast unevangelized regions, came as a daily call to lengthen the cords, while daily study of God's Word for the purposes of translation was a daily lesson in strengthening the stakes.[72]

His journal tells the story of months of hard work on the translation of the New Testament:

April 14: Revision nine hours.

April 15: Ten and a half hours.

April 16: Eight hours.

April 17: Eleven and a half hours.

April 18: Eleven hours

April 19, Sunday: Morning, wrote to James Meadows . . . had service with Lae-djün. Afternoon, took tea with Mr. John Howard having walked to Tottenham to inquire after Miss Stacy's health. Evening, heard Mr. Howard preach. Proposed to Miss Howard, as subjects for prayer, that we should be helped in revision – to do it well and as quickly as is consistent with so doing. Walked home. (12 miles in total.)

April 20: Revision twelve hours.

April 21: Revision eleven hours.

April 22: Revision ten hours.

April 23: Revision twelve hours.

April 24: Revision nine and a half hours.

April 25: Revision thirteen and a half hours.[73]

And, after a few months not distracted by worries over finance, he wrote:

October 5, Monday: Our money nearly spent. Paid in faith, however, what was owing to tradesmen and servants. Found a very sweet promise for us in our revision work, 1 Chron. Xxviii .20. Revision seven hours.

October 9: Money all but gone. O Lord, our hope is in Thee! Revision six and a half hours. Mrs. Jones, Mrs. Lord, May Jones and Baby came from Bristol.

October 10: Revision nine and a half hours . . . Went with Mrs. Jones to see Mr. Jonathan Hutchinson, who kindly refused to take my fee. Only 2s.5½d left, with great management. I must have all things and abound while God is God to me.

October 11, Sunday: Morning, with Lae-djün. Afternoon engaged in prayer. Evening, went to hear Mr. Kennedy. We gave 2s. today to the collections, in faith and as due to the Lord.[74]

Faith for the future

Nothing stopped Hudson Taylor; nothing drew him away from his vision. Lack of money did not, discouragement did not and poor health did not. Even through the darkest hour, when it seemed as though the translation would not be completed at all due to lack of funding, he persevered, believing in the importance of this task.

God provided, often at the last minute, but never too late. These six years in London, the whole life of Hudson Taylor in fact, testified to the wonderful provision of God. Sometimes he had to progress at a much slower pace, but he carried on, and the race was won by the little steps he took each day. Small steps can be difficult sometimes, especially when the enemy throws obstacles your way.

I knew God was speaking. I knew that in answer to prayer evangelists would be given and their support secured, because the Name of Jesus is worthy. But there unbelief came in. 'Suppose the workers are given and go to China: trials will come; their faith may fail; would they not reproach you for bringing them into such a plight? Have you ability to cope with so painful a situation?' And the answer was, of course, a decided negative. It was just a bringing in of self, through unbelief; the devil getting one to feel that while prayer and faith would bring one into the fix, one would have to get out of it as best one might. And I did not see that the Power that would give the men and the means would be sufficient to keep them also, even the far interior of China.

Meanwhile, a million a month were dying in that land, dying without God. This was burned into my soul. For two or three months the conflict was intense. I scarcely slept night or day more than an hour at a time, and feared I should lose my reason. Yet I did not give in.[75]

On 25 June 1865 he visited a conference in Brighton. God spoke in the silence.

Unable to bear the sight of a congregation of a thousand or more Christian people rejoicing in their own security, while millions were perishing for lack of knowledge, I wandered out on the sands alone, in great spiritual agony; and there the Lord conquered my unbelief, and I surrendered myself to God for this service. I told Him that all the responsibility as to issues and consequences must rest with Him; that as His servant, it was mine to obey and to follow Him – His, to direct, to care for, and to guide me and those who might labour with me. Need I say that peace at once flowed into my burdened heart? There and then I asked Him for twenty-four fellow-workers, two for each of eleven inland provinces which were without a missionary, and two for Mongolia; and writing the petition on the margin of the Bible I had with me, I returned home with a heart enjoying rest such as it had been a stranger to for months, and with an assurance that the Lord would bless His own work and that I should share in the blessing. I had previously prayed, and asked prayer, that workers might be raised up for the eleven then unoccupied provinces, and thrust forth and provided for, but had not surrendered myself to be their leader.[76]

This thought came in to the mind of Hudson Taylor and transformed it forever: 'If we are obeying the Lord, the responsibility rests with Him, not with us . . . I go forward leaving results with Thee.'[77]

That day on the beach in Brighton he put down in writing: 'Prayed for twenty-four more missionaries to be given to the work in China.'[78]

Peace followed. Then faith expressed itself in action. Two days later, Hudson Taylor opened an account for the China Inland Mission and paid in ten pounds. The CIM was born – though it had been alive in his heart long before it saw the light of day.

Many days followed in East Grinstead where Hudson Taylor and Maria together with Mr Berger (a Christian starch manufacturer) and his wife prayed and talked over the values and principles of the CIM. They all agreed it should be evangelistic and interdenominational; the level of commitment and relationship with Jesus was far more

important than education: everyone was welcomed no
matter what their class or background; 'the proposed
field is so extensive, and the needs of labourers of every
class is so great, that "the eye cannot say to the hand, I
have no need of thee"; nor yet again the head to the feet,
"I have no need of you." '[79] Ningpo was to become the
Chinese headquarters of the CIM. And although the
name of the organization itself pointed to the inland
province, work was also to be done in Ningpo. Mr Berger
was to take care of running the CIM on the home front in
England. 'It was decided that there should be no collections or authorised appeals for support in order that
funds might not be deflected from other channels.'[80] All
the workers in the field were to adopt Chinese dress.[81]

Sharing the need

In September the same year Hudson Taylor was invited to
a conference in Perth, Scotland. He shared the following
story from one of his Chinese evangelistic trips.

Our boat drew nearer the walls of the city, and I went
into the cabin to prepare for going ashore, expecting in a
few minutes to enter Sung-kiand Fu with my Chinese
friend. I was suddenly startled by a splash and a cry. I
sprang out of the cabin, and looked around – every one
was at his post but poor Peter. The tide was rapidly running out, but a strong wind was carrying us over it. The
low, shrubless shore afforded no landmark that we could
notice to indicate the exact spot where he fell into the
water. I instantly let down the sail and leapt overboard,

trying to find him. Unsuccessful, I looked around in agonizing suspense, and saw close to me a fishing boat with a peculiar drag net furnished with hooks, which I knew would bring him up.

'Come!' I cried, as hope sprang up in my heart, 'Come, and drag over this spot directly, for a man is drowning here.'

'Veh bin' – it's not convenient – was the cold and unfeeling reply.

'Don't talk of convenience,' I cried in an agony, 'a man is drowning.'

'We are busy fishing and cannot come,' was the reply.

'Never mind your fishing,' I cried, 'I will give you more money than many a day's fishing will bring you, if you will come at once.'

'How much money will you give us?'

'Don't stand talking now; do come, or you will be too late. I'll give you five dollars.'

'We won't come for that; we'll drag for twenty dollars.'

'I have not got so much, do come quickly and I'll give you all the money I have.'

'How much is that?'

'I don't know exactly: about fourteen dollars.'

At last they came, and in less than one minute brought up the body of poor Peter. They were most indignant and clamorous because the payment of their exorbitant demand was delayed while attempts were being made at resuscitation. But all was in vain – life was extinct.[82]

Looking at the crowd, he continued:

Is the body, then of so much more value than soul? We condemn those heathen fishermen. We say they were guilty of the man's death – because they could easily have saved him, and did not do it. But what of the millions we leave to perish, and that eternally? What of the plain command, 'Go ye into all the world and preach the Gospel to every creature,' and the searching question inspired by God Himself, 'If thou forbear to deliver them that are drawn unto death and those that are ready to be slain; if thou sayest, Behold, we knew it not, doth not He that pondereth the heart consider it?' And He that keepeth thy soul doth not He know it? And shall He not render to every man according to his works?

Do you believe that each unit of these millions has an immortal soul . . . and that there is none other name under heaven given among men save the precious name of Jesus whereby we must be saved? Do you believe, that He and He alone is the Way, the Truth and the Life, and that no man cometh unto the Father but by Him? If so, think of the condition of these unsaved souls, and examine yourself in the sight of God to see whether you are doing your utmost to make Him known to them or not . . .

It will not do to say that you have no special call to go to China. With these facts before you, you need rather to ascertain whether you have a special call to stay at home. If in the sight of God you cannot say you are sure that you have a special call to stay at home, why are you disobeying the Saviour's plain command to go? Why are you refusing to come to the help of the Lord against the mighty? If, however, it is perfectly clear that duty – not inclination, not pleasure, not business – detains you at home, are you labouring in prayer?[84]

After his step of faith and the appeals for workers, the funding started to slowly trickle in – God also started to bring people to Hudson Taylor who would have a key influence on his future. Busy days of writing followed. Together with Maria, he wrote *China's Spiritual Need and Claims* which required much study. It became a massive encouragement to many, and as a result of its publication, scores of people joined not only CIM but also other missionary agencies. It opened the eyes of western Christians to the need for the evangelization of China. It was thoroughly researched and beautifully illustrated – and was probably the most influential and inspirational nineteenth-century piece of writing on missions.

'Every sentence was steeped in prayer. It grew up while we were writing – I walking up and down the room and Maria seated at the table.'[85]

Mr Berger (who had become the first Home Secretary), one of the most generous supporters of the CIM, paid the first publishing costs of the book.

During this time Maria fell ill again, her physical strength weakened by running the Mission and bringing up four children. Yet once more God's healing hand was upon her.

The current situation was also favourable to Hudson Taylor. In 1859, and the few years after, there was a new awareness of the need for mission, and many people were interested in being used by God overseas. Busy days followed: interviewing candidates, attending meetings and writing correspondence. The CIM began to grow, and a short illustration from Berger was very helpful to them

You must wait for it to grow, before there can be much in the way of branches. First you have only a slender stem with a few leaves or shoots. Then little twigs appear. Ultimately these may become great limbs, all but separate trees: but it takes time and patience. If there is life, it will develop after its own order.[86]

The demands of travel and meetings were so great Hudson Taylor eventually had to stop working on the translation of the New Testament. He spent four-and-a-half years on it; the work was continued by Revd F.F. Gough, and finally completed by Revd George Moule.

At this point he was able to pay a visit to Bristol and meet George Müller, who encouraged him, urging him to always spend time with God no matter how busy the ministry. He spoke on overcoming obstacles and growing in the discipline of prayer and Bible study. Hudson Taylor also had the opportunity to see the orphanages George Müller had opened; they ran on donations that miraculously came when he prayed.

Enlarge the Place of Your Tent

Key learning points

Spiritual Formation

God raises up missionaries by prayer. Hudson Taylor realized he needed to pray rather than make elaborate appeals for labourers.

Discerning Vision

Vision is often born out of dissatisfaction. The CIM came into existence because of the inadequacies of the existing mission societies.

Passion keeps the vision alive. Hudson Taylor's passion for the Chinese never ceased. He saw the situation of the unevangelized areas as an urgent need, this sense of urgency remained constant.

Leadership Skills

God can turn obstacles into opportunities. The forced 'retirement' to England gave Hudson Taylor an opportunity to take a step back and gain a wider view of what needed to be done in China. It enabled him to set up the CIM, which could ultimately have a far greater impact than he could alone.

Share the need. Clearly communicate the need for which you are labouring, and the vision God has set before you: and then trust God to create the response in people's hearts and lives.

Don't be afraid of hard work. Hudson Taylor worked hard and always to a standard of excellence. His methods were creative and innovative.

Be faithful. Persevere with the vision to which God has called you, during both the productive and the difficult seasons.

7

Sowing with Tears

1866–70

The next years of ministry in China would be years of both triumph and despair. Throughout it all, Hudson Taylor remained faithful to the vision he had been given, and the God who had called him.

The Lammermuir Party

By 26 May 1866 the long-awaited dream had come true. After months of countless meetings, much prayer and many interviews with potential missionaries, Hudson Taylor, together with a group of workers, boarded the *Lammermuir* – a tea clipper to take them to China. They set off from the East India Docks in London carrying with them plenty of medicine, apparatus for the hospital, and a printing press. Henceforth, this date, the anniversary of them sailing to China, would be set aside by members of the CIM for prayer and fasting.

Those who went were: James Hudson Taylor, Maria Taylor and their four children (Grace, Herbert, Frederick and Samuel), Lewis Nicol, Mrs Eliza Calder Nicol, George Duncan, Josiah Alexander Jackson, William

David Rudland, John Robert Sell, James Williamson, Susan Barnes, Mary Elizabeth Bausum, Emily Blatchley, Mary Bell, Mary Bowyer, Louise Desgraz, Jane Elizabeth Faulding, Jane McLean, Elisabeth Rose.

Hudson Taylor had asked for 24 missionaries and, together with those who had already gone ahead, their number was exactly 24.

Originally, it was hoped the journey on the ship would bind the team together, and allow more time for learning the language and general preparation for the mission ahead. However, the four-month journey was not an easy one. Seasickness, disharmony amongst the team, and the difficulties involved with learning Chinese seemed, at times, close to tearing the group apart. During the long voyage, although some crew members were led to Christ, a few of the missionaries began acting in an exceptionally unchristian manner. The Lammermuir Party, as they became known, had numerous disputes, sometimes caused by incredibly ridiculous issues. One of these was missing stockings. 'Lewis Nicol discovered that someone had forgotten to pack an extra pair of stockings in his outfit. He had seen a list of articles supplied to the Presbyterian missionaries, and they received better outfits. Taylor apologized and offered to give Lewis a pair of his own stockings, as well as "light clothes" for the tropics. Later Nicol refused to join the communion service in the saloon since the converted sailors were neither baptized nor church members.'[87]

Just before they reached Shanghai a powerful storm broke out and kept them from arriving for a further three weeks. The journey, combined with the disunity, had worn them out. And, when they eventually reached Shanghai, they were not welcomed warmly by everyone. This time, many missionaries already in China representing other organizations criticized Hudson Taylor's approach and leadership. They were troubled by the fact single women had come, that they were to be sent to the interior, and that they wore Chinese clothes. Hudson Taylor already knew about the benefits of adopting Chinese dress, and was not willing to compromise in this area. He believed in culturally relevant evangelism.

I am not alone in the opinion that the foreign dress and carriage of missionaries (to a certain extent effected by some of their pupils and converts), the foreign appearance of chapels and indeed the foreign air imparted to everything connected with their work has seriously hindered the rapid dissemination of the Truth among the Chinese. And why should such a foreign aspect be given to Christianity? The Word of God does not require it; nor, I conceive, could sound reason justify it. It is not the denationalization but the Christianization of this people that we seek. We wish to see Chinese Christians raised up – men and women truly Christian, but withal truly Chinese in every right sense of the word. We wish to see churches of such believers presided over by pastors and officers of their own countrymen, worshipping God in the land of their fathers, in their own tongue, and in edifices of a thoroughly native style of architecture . . . Let us adopt their dress, acquire their language, seek to conform to their habits and approximate to their diet as far as health and constitution will allow. Let us live in their houses, making no unnecessary alteration in external form, and only so far modifying their internal arrangements as health and efficiency for work absolutely require.[88]

The operations of the Mission were from the first both systematic and methodical. As the Apostle Paul sought to establish churches in the great strategic centres of the Roman Empire, so Mr. Taylor recognized the importance of gaining a footing, if practical, in the provincial capitals, though these were the most difficult places in which to found churches. With the provincial capitals opened, the next step was to open a station in the chief prefecture, and thus downwards to the smaller towns and villages.[89]

Their first target capital was Hangchow, about two hundred miles from Shanghai in the province of Chekiang. They all travelled, just as Hudson Taylor had done on so many occasions, in house boats.

Trying circumstances

After finding a place to live, an almost impossible task, they settled to learning the language, and kept a low profile for a while to allow the locals to get accustomed to their presence before proceeding with any missionary work. Soon, though, the discord and muttering that had started during the sea voyage intensified. It was a mixture of factors: Hudson Taylor's insistence on wearing Chinese dress and eating Chinese food, together with living conditions far harder than many had imagined. The names of those causing trouble are never mentioned in the book by Howard Taylor, but they were thorny and fractious individuals who almost drove the CIM to its end. They undermined Hudson Taylor's authority and rejected the rules of the mission to which they had been introduced before leaving England. They wrote letters and tried to discredit the work to the supporters. Throughout all this time Hudson and Maria Taylor acted with integrity and discretion. Maria wanted to share her sorrow with Mrs Berger but was asked not to by her husband. Instead, just a few months after landing in China with the Lammermuir Party, she wrote:

Oh, if you were here, how your heart would grieve! But we must not be surprised, must we, at troubles and offences coming, and severe sorrows too? This work was not undertaken with the expectation that it would be free from difficulties. And our God who has hitherto helped us and has brought us thus far, who was with us in the typhoon and delivered us from the jaws of death, will surely be with our Mission in the storm, delivering it too from shipwreck.[90]

He did not fail them in the midst of conflict and the birth pains of the mission but was a refuge during the times of trouble.

Adding to these problems was a tragedy in their family. One of the most trying moments was the death of their first child Gracie on 15 August 1867, only a year after their arrival to China. She died of meningitis.

> I know not how to write to you, nor how to refrain. I seem to be writing almost from the inner chamber of the King of Kings – surely this is holy ground. I am striving to write a few lines from the side of a couch on which my darling little Gracie lies dying . . . Dear Brother, our flesh and heart may fail, but God is the strength of our heart and our portion forever. It was no vain nor unintelligent act, when knowing the land, its people, and climate, I laid my dear wife and the darling children with myself on the altar of his service.[91]

Much distress, in China and at home, was caused by illness of team members and continuous back-biting. The troubles at many stations required on Hudson Taylor's part long days of travel, conflict resolution skills and much grace. After facing prolonged distress from a small group of missionaries (who eventually left the CIM) Hudson Taylor outlined to Mr Berger the requirements for a candidate for mission.

> It is most important that married missionaries should be double missionaries – not half or a quarter or eight-part

missionaries. Might we not with advantage say to our candidates: our work is a peculiar one? We aim at the interior, where the whole of society will be Chinese. If you wish for luxury and freedom from care . . . do not join us. Unless you intend your wife to be a true missionary, not merely a wife, home-maker, and friend, do not join us. She must be able to read and be master of at least one Gospel in colloquial Chinese before you marry. A person of ordinary ability may accomplish this in six months, but if she needs longer there is the more reason to wait until she has reached this point before you marry. She must be prepared to be happy among Chinese when the duties of your calling require, as they often will, your temporary absence from home. You, too, must master the initial difficulties of the language and open up a station, if none be allotted to you before you marry. With diligence and God's blessing you may hope to do this in a year or so. If these conditions seem too hard, these sacrifices too great to make for perishing in China, do not join our Mission. These are small things to some of the crosses you may be permitted to bear for your dear Master! China is not to be won for Christ by self-seeking, ease-loving men and women. Those not prepared for labour, self-denial, and many discouragements will be poor helpers in the work. In short, the men and women we need are those who will put Jesus, China, souls first and foremost in everything and at all times: life itself must be secondary – nay, even those more precious than life. Of such men, of such women, do not fear to send us too many. Their price is far above rubies.[92]

Despite all the attacks the CIM was growing. It became a unique missionary movement of its time: ecumenical, accepting missionaries not on their education but on their spirituality, and employing single women for the cause of the gospel. The latter was the most controversial aspect of the CIM, but the fruit of the missions led by women was indisputable. Several volumes could be written just to tell the stories of the many brave female missionaries who first ventured into inland China despite numerous dangers.

> Do pray for us very much, for we do so need God's prevailing grace at the present time. We have come to fight Satan in his very strongholds, and he will not let us alone. What folly were ours, were we here in our own strength! But greater is He that is for us than all that are against us. One is sometimes tempted to feel overwhelmed with Satan's power here; but our God will not fail nor forsake us.[93]

Their troubles were not only multiplying in China: painful news of further criticism came also from England.

> My earnest prayer to God is that you may not be further moved by the letter than the Lord would have you be; and may He give the right spirit and the wisdom that will enable us both to do that which will please Him. The difficulties at home are neither few nor slight, but yours are truly mountainous. You need our every sympathy and

prayer; and be sure, my dear Brother, whatever Mr. ---
may have penned, you hold the same place in our hearts
as before. That God will supply you and me with increasing wisdom and ability for the work to which He has
called us, we need neither fear nor doubt. All that is
required on our part is to lay aside everything we discover to be either faulty or erroneous, and constantly to be
adding to our stock of both wisdom and love. O yes! We
will commit this matter to the Lord who knows that we
did our best. He is very pitiful and will never leave nor
forsake us in this our time of trial.

Yangchow riot

Native hatred of foreigners was on the rise again. One of
the female missionaries wrote describing the events of
that time:

For the last few days we have been almost in a state of
siege. Mr. Taylor, just up from a sick-bed and weak as he
is, has hardly dared to leave the gate. Messrs. Reid and
Rudland with him, and on Saturday night Mr. Duncan
opportunely arrived. Happily, before the disturbances
became very serious, we were able by pressing on the
workman to get the many entrances into our wandering
premises contracted into one . . . But our trust is not in the
walls we build, which an infuriated mob could easily
overthrow . . . but under the shadow of His wings.

The most calumnious hand-bills against us have been
posted about the city. In one of them the Name of Jesus is

blasphemed in the vilest terms, and the paper professes to emanate from the god of war, Kwan-ti. Today (Tuesday) was placarded as the day for attacking our house and setting it in on fire, regardless of native or foreign occupants. Once or twice the mob has seemed inclined to break in by force, but the disturbance is less than on Sunday. God is with us, we do not fear . . . We know that whatever happens will be by His permission, for we have put ourselves in His hands. He will not leave us. As I write He is sending thunder and the threatening of rain, which will do more for us, Mr. Taylor was saying, than an army of soldiers. The Chinese shun rain; the most important matters they will postpone on account of it. May God forgive these poor blind people, and defeat Satan, by making these disturbances the means of more widely diffusing the truth among them. 'Surely the wrath of man shall praise Thee; and the remainder of wrath Thou shall restrain.' Any attempt to set the place on fire now would be vain indeed, for the rain is coming down in torrents.[95]

Things seemed to calm for a short while, but then a couple of white missionaries from Chin-kiang came to visit Yangchow (where Hudson Taylor and his team were based) and they wore very distinctive English outfits. Again, the outfits proved to be the proverbial straw that broke the camel's back. Soon after the two foreigners left rumours spread that 24 children were missing, and had apparently been kidnapped by English. Anger against foreigners intensified; those who had remained were forced to flee, only narrowly escaping death as the mob entered and plundered their homes. Homeless, bruised and unfairly accused, they still hoped one day to be able to return.

They all hid in nearby Chin-kiang. However, one of the hosts reported the events of the previous days to a Shanghai paper. Though not intending any harm, the British authorities sent gunboats, and this almost led to war and caused considerable difficulties back in England. 'The attention the subject evoked and the prejudice displayed were extraordinary. From the "connected narrative" in *The Times* of December 1, "explaining" the whole situation, to the discussion in the House of Lords on March 9 – in which, after a heated declaration, the Duke of Somerset urged that all British missionaries should be recalled from China – the matter seems hardly to have been absent from the public mind.'[96] Hudson Taylor was uncomfortable with the way it had all happened, for he would never have reported it to the papers, believing in God's protection and justice on their behalf. Now the situation was very awkward, and many untrue stories were in circulation, resulting in increased correspondence, but a significant decrease in funding, as some of the supporters pulled out. During this time, when some stopped giving or gave less, George Müller increased his financial support.

He had been sending regularly to several members of the Mission sometimes as much as twenty-five pounds a quarter; and now, within a day or two of the Yang-chow riot (long before he heard of it), he wrote to Mr. Berger asking for the names of others who were thoroughly satisfactory in their work whom he might add to his list. Mr. Berger sent him six names from which to choose, and his choice was to take them all.[97]

My dear Brother, [George Müller wrote in October] the work of the Lord in China is more and more laid on my heart, and hence I have been longing and praying to be able to assist it more and more with means, as well as with prayer. Of late I have especially had a desire to help all the dear brethren and sisters with you with pecuniary means. This I desired especially that they might see that I was interested in them all. This desire the Lord has fulfilled, and I now send you a cheque for £10 for Miss Blatchley, £10 for Miss Bowyer, £10 for Miss Desgraz, £25 for Mr. Harvey, £25 for Mr. C. T. Fishe, £25 for Mr. Reid, £25 for Mr. Jackson, £25 for Mr. Stott, £25 for Mr. Ed. Fishe, £25 for Mr. Rudland, £25 for Mr. Cordon. Be pleased to convey these cheques to each, with the request to acknowledge the receipt of the amount.

Likewise – I enclose a letter for all the dear brethren and sisters connected with the China Inland Mission. May I ask you, dear Brother, to let it be read by all who are now with you; and would you kindly have it copied out for those who are not with you, to send it to them with their money. I feel how I burden you; but I think it would be a service to the Lord to let the dear brethren and sisters see, individually, how interested I am in them.[98]

My chief object is to tell you that I love you in the Lord; that I feel deeply interested about the Lord's work in China, and that I pray daily for you. I thought it might be a little encouragement to you in your difficulties, trials, hardships and disappointments to hear of one more who felt for you and who remembered you before the Lord. But were it otherwise, had you even no one to care for you, or did you at least seem to be in a position as if no one cared for you, you will always have the Lord to be with you. Remember Paul's case at Rome (2 Tim. 4:16-18). On Him then reckon, to Him look, on Him depend; and be assured, if you walk with Him and look to Him, and expect help from Him, He will never fail you. An older brother, who has known the Lord forty-four years, who writes this, says to you for your encouragement that He has never failed him. In the greatest difficulties, in the heaviest trials, in the deepest poverty and necessities, He has never failed me; but, because I was enabled by His grace to trust in Him, He has always appeared for my help. I delight in speaking well of His Name.[99]

Howard Taylor adds: 'Mr. Müller's gifts for the next few years amounted to nearly £2000 annually. In 1870 he sent Mr. Taylor £1940. He was now largely assisting twenty-one missionaries, who with twelve wives constituted the entire staff of the Mission; thirty-three, including Mr. and Mrs. Taylor.'[100]

I have often asked you to remember me in prayer . . . and when I have done so there has been much need of it. That need has never been greater than at the present time. Envied by some, despised by many, hated perhaps by others; often blamed for things I never heard of, or had nothing to do with; an innovator on what have become established rules of missionary practice; an opponent of mighty systems of heathen error and superstition; working without precedent in many respects, and with few experienced helpers; often sick in body, as well as perplexed in mind and embarrassed by circumstances, had not the Lord been specially gracious to me, had not my mind been sustained by the conviction that the work is His, and that He is with me in what it is no empty figure to call 'the thick of the conflict'; I must have fainted and broken down. But the battle is the Lord's: and He will conquer. We may fail, do fail continually; but He never fails. Still I need your prayers more than ever before.

My own position becomes continually more and more responsible and my need greater of special grace to fill it; but I have continually to mourn that I follow at such a distance and learn so slowly to imitate my precious Master. I cannot tell you how I am buffeted sometimes by temptation. I never knew how bad a heart I had. Yet I do know that I love God and love His work, and desire to serve Him only and in all things. And I value above all things that precious Saviour in Whom alone I can be accepted. Often I am tempted to think that one so full of sin cannot be a child of God at all; but I try to throw it back, and rejoice all the more in the preciousness of Jesus, and in the riches of that grace that has made us, accepted in the Beloved. Beloved He is of God; beloved He ought to be of us. But oh, how short I fall here again! May God help me to love him more and serve Him better. Do pray for me. Pray that Lord will keep me from sin, will sanctify me wholly, and will use me more largely in His service.[101]

And the Lord answered his prayer. A new sense of belonging and abiding came upon Hudson Taylor as he meditated upon the verses from the fifteenth chapter of the Gospel of John. This deepening of faith was necessary in order for him to face the even greater trials lying ahead. The sense of abiding was important in a difficult time for their family. Because of the poor health of all the children, exposed to the harshness of Chinese climate, they considered sending them back to England, apart from Charles (who had been born only recently). It was not an easy decision but it seemed the right one. Emily Bletchley, not well herself, offered to take care of the children and accompany them back to England. Maria was to stay behind in China as the needs of the mission were pressing. Tragically, a few months later, their little boy, Samuel, suffering from tuberculosis enteritis, died on the river Yangtze before he was able to return to England.

Among the personal tragedies, there was also no end to the troubles on the political scene.

Politically, we are facing a crisis . . . If our Government continues their present, I had almost said mad policy, war must result. In the mean time our position is becoming always more embarrassing . . . You can scarcely judge how intricate our path seems at times.[102]

We had previously known something of trial in one station or another . . . but now in all simultaneously, or nearly so, a wide-spread excitement shook the very foundations of native society. It is impossible to describe the alarm and consternation of the Chinese, when first they believed that native magicians were bewitching them, or their indignation and anger when told that these insidious foes were the agents of foreigners. It is well known how in Tien-tsin they rose and barbarously murdered the Romish Sisters of Charity, the priests, and even the French Consul. What then restrained them in the interior, where our brothers were alone, far from any protecting human power? Nothing but the mighty hand of God, in answer to united, constant prayer, offered in the all-prevailing name of JESUS. And this same power kept us satisfied with Jesus – with His presence, His love, His providence.[103]

One difficulty follows another very fast . . . but God reigns, not chance.[104]

Personal tragedy

On 7 July 1870, only a few months after Samuel's death, Maria gave birth to their fifth son, Noel. The baby boy did not survive past a fortnight. And, soon after the death of his tiny son, Hudson Taylor was attending to his beloved wife and companion. Maria was very ill: she, like Samuel, also had tuberculosis enteritis.

At daybreak on Saturday the 23rd of July, she was sleeping quietly, and Mr. Taylor left her a few moments to prepare some food. While he was doing so she awoke, and serious symptoms called him to her side.

'By this time it was dawn,' he wrote, 'and the sunlight revealed what the candle had hidden – the deathlike hue of her countenance. Even my love could no longer deny, not her danger, but that she was actually dying. As soon as I was sufficiently composed, I said "My darling, do you know that you are dying?" "Dying!" she replied. "Do you think so? What makes you think so?" I said, "I can see it, darling. Your strength is giving way." "Can it be so? I feel no pain, only weariness." "Yes, you are going Home. You will soon be with Jesus." My precious wife thought of my being left alone at a time of so much trial, with no companion like herself, with whom I had been wont to bring every difficulty to the Throne of Grace. "I am so sorry," she said, and paused as if half correcting herself for the feeling. "You are not sorry to go to be with Jesus?" Never shall I forget the look with which she answered, "Oh, no! It is not that. You know, darling, that for ten years past there has not been a cloud between me and my Saviour. I cannot be sorry to go to Him; but it does grieve me to leave you alone at such a time. Yet . . . He will be with you and meet all your need."

But little was said after that. A few loving messages to those at home, a few last words about the children, and she seemed to fall asleep or drift into unconsciousness of earthly things. The summer sun rose higher and higher over the city, the hills, and the river. The busy hum of life came up around them from many a court and street. But within one Chinese dwelling, in an upper room from which the blue of God's own heaven could be seen, there was the hush of a wonderful peace.[105]

Though sustained by God in his bereavement, Hudson Taylor missed her and the children desperately. He often thought of those days when, even though he had to travel somewhere far away, he always had a place to go back to; a home, full of the warmth of loved ones. He felt greatly lonely again. 'I feel like a person stunned with a blow or recovering from a faint' he wrote in one of his letters.[106] He was suffering from a liver infection which kept him in bed and feeling exhausted. Furthermore, the little baby boy, Charles, who was still with him, was battling for his own life.

'Long-continued anxiety and weariness from want of rest, sorrow from repeated bereavements and trouble in the work, from the state of China and the timidity of the workers, and other trials from without and within do make one feel the need of a strong arm to lean on – aye, and a tender one too.'[107]

Sowing with Tears

Key learning points

Spiritual Formation

Cling on to God. During the many deaths and tragedies, Hudson Taylor would not have been able to carry on were it not for the depth of his relationship and reliance on God. Look to God for your support, your protection and your vindication.

Leadership Skills

Focus on the big picture. Ridiculous disputes threatened the unity of the Lammermuir Party. Encourage team members to see the worth of pursuing the vision, so as to minimize arguments over minor issues.

Don't discriminate. Hudson Taylor accepted single women and uneducated men to become missionaries. God calls all people, not simply those who are similar to ourselves.

Take time to plan. The expansion of the work was strategically thought through. Prayerful planning allows for more to be achieved.

Mission Skills

Believe in those you are serving. Hudson Taylor's desire to see a totally Chinese church, Chinese leaders, and Chinese styles of worship, architecture, etc., was far ahead of his time, and showed his deep understanding of the gospel, and his belief in the potential of his Chinese converts.

8

Fearless and Invincible

1870–74

During his darkest days of bereavement, illness and lack of funds, Hudson Taylor continued to place all of his hope in God. So it was during that period he felt the presence of God most profoundly in his life.

A man of grief

How lonesome, were the weary hours when confined to my room. How I missed my dear wife and the little pattering footsteps of the children far away in England! Then it was I understood why the Lord had made that passage so real to me, 'Whosoever drinketh of the water that I shall give him shall never thirst.' Twenty times a day, perhaps, as I felt the heart-thirst coming back, I cried to Him 'Lord, you promised! You promised me that I should never thirst.'[108]

At times He does suffer me to realize all that was, but is not now. At times I can almost hear again the sweet voice of my Gracie; feel the presence of little Samuel's head on my bosom. And Noel and his mother – how sweet the recollection, and yet how it makes the heart ache! . . . And then, He who will soon come and wipe away every tear comes and takes all bitterness from them . . . and fills my heart with deep, true, unutterable gladness. I have not to seek Him now; He never leaves me. At night He smoothes my pillow; in the morning He wakes my heart to His love. 'I will be with thee all day: thou shalt not be alone, nor lonely.' I never was so happy, dear Mrs. Berger, I know you sympathize, and I feel I must tell you of His love. It is of JESUS I would speak. He brings a poor, vile sinner into His house of wine.[109]

Back at home in England, George Müller was also grieving the loss of his wife. The two friends comforted each other through letters.

You do know, beloved Brother, what the cup is that I am daily called to drink – yes, many times every day. You know that it does not become less bitter, nor is the lack of help less felt as days run on into weeks and weeks into months. And you know too how His grace can make one glad to have such a cup from His hand, or any other cup He may be pleased to give. Yet the flesh is weak; and your sympathy and prayers I do prize and thank you for. They tell me of Him Who, when the poor and needy seek water and there is none – no, not one drop – opens rivers in high places and fountains in the midst of the valleys.[110]

Hudson Taylor was under constant strain due to work, mountains of correspondence and poor health. 'A badly deranged liver made him sleepless and brought on painful physical depression. This was increased by lung trouble which caused not only pain but serious difficulty in breathing. His suffering condition made him the more conscious of outward loneliness, yet in it all he was proving the sustaining power of the Word of God.'[111]

Finally, in 1872, he was forced to return to England again. He travelled back on a ship with Jennie Faulding, who had first come to China on board the *Lammermuir* in 1866. She was soon to become his second wife and an amazing help to his ministry.

Regrouping at home

On arrival, he learned the CIM Home Secretary, Mr Berger, had decided to retire. Both Mr and Mrs Berger had served the CIM faithfully for many years, giving their time, expertise, prayer and financial support to the mission, but now they were moving to Cannes in southern France. It was impossible to think of how they could be replaced. Therefore, during his time of grief, Hudson Taylor had to consider how to restructure the CIM at home.

A Council of Reference was formed, including such notable people as Thomas Barnardo, Robert Chapman of Barnstaple, Grattan Guinness, George Müller, Williams Pennefather and Lord Radstock.

Another important step was to create the London Council, a team of people to look after affairs at home; Richard Hill and Henry Soltau were appointed honorary secretaries of this council. Emily Blatchley, who was looking after Hudson Taylor's children, was also now charged with organizing prayer meetings and taking care of the missionaries coming back to England. The council had a treasurer, a company director and someone responsible for training.[112] (In 1883, ten years after the creation of the London Council, Hudson Taylor would encourage the creation of a China Council, an idea rejected by some. It caused a massive crisis within the ranks of the CIM in England, with some members afraid of losing power.)

Even though the funding had fallen greatly after Berger's retirement, Hudson Taylor was planning for even more expansion of the mission in China. He again asked for 18 people to be sent.

After bringing the home issues to some sort of order, he departed for China for the third time, this time with his new wife, Jennie. They arrived in April 1872, to mixed news of both encouragement and distress. They found some stations in need of supervision, missionaries forced to abandon their posts, widespread sickness, and backsliding, even sin, in some of the Chinese workers. The latter was mainly due to a lack of discipleship. Hudson Taylor started visiting the mission stations, encouraging the foreign and native workers.

I should tremble indeed, had we not God to look to, at the prospect of being so soon face to face with the difficulties of the work. Even as it is, I can scarcely help feeling oppressed. 'Lord, increase my faith.' Do pray earnestly for me. One more unworthy there could not be. And oh, how I feel my utter incapacity – to carry on the work aright! May the mighty God of Jacob ever be my help . . . . I can form no conception as to what our course may be, or whether it will take us N., S., E., or W. I never felt so fully and utterly cast on the Lord but in due time He will lead us on.[113]

He hoped the situation would again improve, and pressed on despite the difficulties: 'May the Lord give us his blessing. Though times are very sadly, they are not hopeless; they will soon look up, with God's blessing, if looked after.'[114]

Building a Chinese team

Hudson Taylor's desire was always to train and release native Chinese workers. His strategy was to remove the 'scaffolding' of foreign missionaries and enable the whole mission to be run by the Chinese. 'His eventual aim was to have one superintendent and two assistant foreign missionaries in a province, with Chinese helpers in each important city, and colporteurs (Bible distributors) in the less important places. He hoped that before the end of 1873 he would be able to open a college to train Chinese workers'[115]

Hudson and Jennie Taylor did not waste a moment. They travelled as often as they could, visiting different stations, writing letters, looking after the sick and encouraging the downhearted. Soon they were able to testify:

The Lord is prospering us and the work is steadily growing, especially in the most important department, native help. The helpers themselves need much help, much care and instruction; but they are becoming more efficient as well as more numerous, and the future hope in China lies, doubles, in them. I look on foreign missioners as the scaffolding round a rising building; the sooner it can be dispensed – or rather, the sooner it can be transferred to other places, to serve the same temporary purpose. As to difficulties and sorrows, their name is legion. Some spring from the nature of the work, some from the nature of the workers. Here Paul and Barnabas cannot see eye to eye; there Peter so acts as to need public rebuke; while elsewhere exhortation is needed to restore a wanderer or quicken one growing cold . . . But it is the Lord's work, and we go on from day to day. He is competent to meet all the matters that may arise, as and when they crop up.[116]

They spent much time serving the missionaries; here Hudson Taylor's medical knowledge proved a blessing because many were ill and physically exhausted. They were committed to the training of native workers and continued to cheer those in every station. To one of the new missionaries who joined the CIM he wrote:

Do not be afraid of His training school. He both knows His scholars, as to what they are, and he knows for what service they are to be fitted. A jeweller will take more pains over a gem than over a piece of glass; but the one he takes most pains over is longer under discipline and most severely dealt with. Once finished, however, the burnish never tarnishes, the brightness never dims. So with us. If we are purified, at times, as in a furnace, it is not merely for earthly service, it is for eternity. May you so appreciate the plans of the Master that you can triumphantly glory in the love that subjects you to such discipline, though the discipline itself be sharp and to flesh hard to bear . . .[117]

Continuous suffering

In April 1873, Jennie gave birth to stillborn twins. The news from home was not positive either. This time, Emily Blatchley, who was doing so much on the 'home front', leading prayer meetings, sending out the *Occasional Paper* (the CIM Prayer letter) was not well at all, and her strength was failing fast.

The finances were low, very low. At that point, Hudson Taylor already had 170 people in his care, comprising of foreign and native workers together with all the children – so even one month with no income for general usage was extremely challenging.

> The one thing we need is to know God. Not in ourselves, not in our prospects, not in heaven itself are we to rejoice, but in the Lord. If we know Him, then we rejoice in what He gives not because we like it, if pleasing, not because we think it will work good, if trying, but because it is His gift, His ordering; and the like in what he withholds and takes away. Oh, to know Him![118]

Not only were the finances short, but so were recruits. This drove Hudson Taylor to train more local leaders, and build a local team. 'I am aiming at such organisation of our forces as will enable us to do more work with fewer foreign missionaries . . . I hope I may be able, ere the year closes, to commence a college for the more thorough training of our native helpers. Long desired, there seems more probability of our attaining this than heretofore.'[119]

He was juggling many difficult balls requiring immediate attention: there were buildings to keep, families of missionaries to feed, lengthy enforced separations from his wife, and then his own children back in England. Who would look after them, now that Emily was not well? However, in the midst of all these worries he still could see clearly what needed to be done. He knew the success of the Mission, its growth and endurance, depended on the local labourers.

We are going into the interior . . . There is great difficulty in conveying much luggage, and the sight of it, in many places, would ensure robbery. If anyone is not prepared to rough it, he had better stay at home at once . . . the only persons wanted here are those who will rejoice to work – really to labour, not to dream their lives away, to deny themselves; to *suffer* in order to *save*.[120]

In 1874, during the Chinese winter, and after a great deal of travelling, he fell seriously ill due to physical exhaustion.

Week after week he lay in helplessness and suffering, able to do nothing but wait upon the Lord. Of all that in his providence was drawing near, Hudson Taylor was unconscious. He only knew that God had given him to see something of the purposes of His heart; that he was sharing in some measure the compassions of Christ for the lost and perishing, and that the love of which he felt the yearnings was His Own infinite love. That that love, that purpose, would find a way to bless, he could not doubt. So he just prayed on – holding in faith to the heavenly vision; ready to go forward when and as the Lord should open the way. Never had advance seemed less possible.[121]

It took several months of rest and waiting on the Lord before he was back in the full swing of work again, and during this time finances dropped even lower. In a letter to his wife he wrote: '"The balance in hand yesterday was sixty-seven cents! The Lord reigns: herein is our joy and confidence." And to Mr. Baller he added, when the balance was still lower, "we have this, and all the promises of God."'[122]

Never has our work entailed such real trial or so much exercise of faith. The sickness of our beloved sister, Miss Blatchley, and her strong desire to see me; the needs of our dear children; the state of the funds; the changes required in the work to admit of some going home, others coming out, and of further expansion, and many other things not easily expressed in writing would be crushing anxieties if we were to bear them. But the Lord bears us and them too, and makes our hearts so very glad in Himself – not Himself plus a bank balance – that I have never known greater freedom from anxiety and care.[123]

Emily Blatchley passed away on 26 July 1874. She was an amazing woman of God, who served the mission wholeheartedly and raised the children with love and wisdom. Hudson Taylor was once again forced to leave China.

Fearless and Invincible

Key learning points

Spiritual Formation

Have a ministry-friend. The correspondence with George Müller helped Hudson Taylor through some of his most challenging periods. Have a friend who understands ministry and leadership challenges, who will pray for you, and who you can share anything with.

Leadership Skills

Develop good structures. The London Council, and the later China Council, gave the CIM good layers of support and supervision at home and in the field. The structures were created to fit around the needs of CIM, not the other way round.

Build an excellent team. The Council of Reference was made up of some of the greatest missionaries and spiritual leaders of the age. Their advice and backing would be invaluable to the CIM.

Invest in people. Be an available leader and mentor, to encourage, discipline, model the way, etc., to the followers God entrusts to you. Hudson Taylor travelled China to visit and encourage the different missionaries and mission stations.

Look after your people. Hudson Taylor's medical knowledge allowed for the missionaries to receive competent treatment.

Mission Skills

Think long term regarding mission. Raising up local leaders became a key objective. The foreign missionaries were only scaffolding. Never forget that the purpose of foreign missions is to build capacity in a nation, so they can stand unsupported as soon as possible.

9

The Cross Does Not Get Comfortable

1874–90

The China Inland Mission continued to send more missionaries to China, and expanded to America, Australia and beyond. Hudson Taylor criss-crossed the whole world to share his passion for the needs of China with as wide an audience as possible.

Working through illness

The same year Emily Blatchley passed away, Hudson Taylor was again bound to his bed; he could hardly lie there comfortably, and, at times, could not even hold a pen. A few months before, while travelling on a cargo boat on the River Yangtze back in China, he had fallen, and, as a consequence, suffered a continuous worsening of his condition; first a sprained ankle, then a gradual paralysis of the legs that incapacitated him for many months. Lying in his room, simultaneously his study and the office of CIM, he prayed for eighteen more missionaries to join him in the evangelization of China.

Jennie was working relentlessly to keep everything moving in the right direction. She herself was pregnant again.

His plans of hard work and accomplishing much while back in England were shattered but God was working on his behalf. Even in this condition Hudson Taylor did not forget the needs of China, and he did not put his vision on hold, even though he could do so little in human terms. At the end of 1875, he wrote, or rather dictated, *Appeal for Prayer* on behalf of more than a hundred and fifty million Chinese people.

It briefly stated the facts with regard to the nine unopened provinces; that friends of C.I.M. had long been praying for men to go as pioneer evangelists to these regions; that recently four thousand pounds had been given for the purpose; and that among the converts in the older stations of the mission were some from the far interior, who were earnestly desiring to carry the Gospel to the districts from which they had come. It did not say that the leader of the Mission was to all appearances a hopeless invalid. It did not refer to the fact that four thousand pounds recently given had come from his wife and himself, part of their capital, the whole of which they had consecrated to the work of God. It did not mention that for two and a half years they and others had been praying daily for the eighteen evangelists, praying in faith.[124]

Soon after the *Appeal for Prayer:*

The eighteen men asked of God began to come. There was first some correspondence; then they came to see me in my room. Soon I had a class studying Chinese at my bedside. In due time the Lord sent them forth and then the dear friends at Mildmay began to pray for my restoration. The Lord blessed the means used and I was raised up. One reason for my being laid aside was gone. Had I been well and able to move about some might have thought that my urgent appeals rather than God's working had sent the eighteen men to China. But utterly laid aside, able only to dictate a request for prayer, the answer to our prayers was the more apparent . . . One of the happiest periods of my life was that period of forced inactivity, when one could do nothing but 'rejoice in the Lord and wait patiently for Him', and see Him meeting all one's need. Never were my letters, before or since, kept so regularly and promptly answered.[125]

Requirements for missionaries

The response to the *Appeal for Prayer* was indeed great. Sixty applicants showed an interest in being missionaries but the requirements set out by Hudson Taylor were clear.

While thankful for any educational advantages that candidates may have enjoyed, we attach far greater importance to spiritual qualifications. We desire men who believe that there is a God and that He is both intelligent and faithful, and who therefore trust Him; who believe that He is the

Rewarder of those who diligently seek Him, and are therefore men of prayer. We desire men who believe the Bible is the Word of God, and who, accepting the declaration 'all power is given unto me' are prepared to carry out to the best of their ability the command, 'Go . . . teach all nations', relying on Him who possesses 'all power' and has promised to be with His messengers 'always' rather than on foreign gun-boats though they possess some power; men who are prepared, therefore, to go to the remotest parts of the interior of China, expecting to find His arm a sufficient strength and stay. We desire men who believe in eternity and live for it; who believe in its momentous issues whether to the saved or to the lost, and therefore cannot but seek and pluck the ignorant and the guilty as brands from the burning.

The mission is supported by donations, not subscriptions. We have, therefore, no guaranteed income, and can only minister to our missionaries as we ourselves are ministered to by God. We do not send men to China as our agents. But men who believe that God has called them to work, who go there to labour for God, and can therefore trust Him Who's they are and Whom they serve to supply their temporal needs, we gladly co-operate with – providing, if needful, outfit and passage money, and such a measure of support as circumstances call for and we are enabled to supply. As may be seen from the last *Occasional Paper* (No. 39), our faith is sometimes tried; but God always proves Himself faithful, and at the right time and in the right way supplies all our need. One-third of the human family are in China, needing the Gospel. Twelve millions there are passing beyond the reach of that Gospel every year. If you want hard work and little appreciation; if you value God's approval more than you fear man's disapprobation; if you are prepared to take joyfully the spoiling of your goods and seal your testimony, if need be, with your blood; if you can pity and love the poor Chinese in all their mental and moral degradation, as well as literal filth and impurity, you may count on a harvest of souls now and a crown of glory hereafter 'that fadeth not away' and on the Master's 'well done.'

You would find that, in connection with the China Inland Mission, it is no question of 'making the most of both worlds.' The men, the only men who will be happy with us, are those who have this world under their feet: and I do venture to say that such men will find a happiness they never dreamed of or thought possible down here. For to those who count 'all things' but dross and dung for 'the excellency of the knowledge of Christ Jesus our Lord', He does manifest Himself in such sort that they are not inclined to rue their bargain. If, after prayerfully considering the matter, you still feel drawn to engage in such work, I shall be only too glad to hear from you again.[126]

The same year (1875), Hudson Taylor, believing the team of eighteen missionaries and the work in China needed a 'more adequate representation', set out to produce an innovative and colourful pamphlet called *China's Millions*. It was a huge enterprise, especially for someone still largely confined to bed, and, at that time, creative, colourful magazines were not particularly popular. All the work of editing and distribution took place from Hudson Taylor's room. The aim was to make the people and the needs of China more real to the reader in far-away England; however, in due course, *China's Millions* also became a powerful source of information about, and thus a weapon against, the opium trade.

The opium trade was for the CIM, as for most missionaries, a moral question, a blot on the national righteousness of England. *China's Millions* played all the themes of the anti-opium crusade. Hardly a month passed without some tragic vignette of opium suicides, emaciated bodies, or scholars reduced to penury. Some reports were so detailed a historian could use them to reconstruct the opium trails of a century ago.[127]

At this point, hatred of foreigners in China was on the rise again and the situation for the missionaries was troubled.

Expanding the vision

It was nine years on the 26th of May since the Lammermuir party sailed for China . . . We have needed all the time since then to gain experience and to gather round us a staff of native workers, through whose aid we are occupying some fifty stations and out-stations in five provinces. We believe, however, that the time has come for doing more fully what the master commanded us; and by His grace we intend to do it – not to try, for we see no scriptural authority for trying. 'Try' is a word constantly on the lips of unbelievers. 'We must do what we can,' they say, and too often the same attitude is taken up of the child of God. In our experience, to try has usually meant to fail. The Lord's word in reference to His various commands is not 'do your best' but 'do it'; that is, do the thing commanded. We are therefore making arrangements for commencing work in each of these nine provinces – without haste, for 'he that believeth shall not make haste' but also without unnecessary delay . . . 'if ye be willing and obedient, ye shall eat of the good of the land.' 'Whatsoever He saith unto you do it.'[128]

Howard Taylor writes about the anniversary of the departure of the Lammermuir Party, held in spring 1876.

Taylor was by this time well enough to move about with the help of a strong walking-stick, and it was with joy that he pointed out on the large map twenty-eight stations in five provinces in which churches had been gathered – 600 converts having been baptised from the beginning. Of these, more than seventy were devoting their lives to making known the Gospel, and in them lay the chief hope of the future, especially in regard to the evangelisation of the unreached interior. Sixty-eight missionaries had been sent to China, of whom fifty-two were still connected with the Mission . . . Without a collection or an appeal of any kind for funds, fifty-two thousand had been raised, and the Mission was not and never had been in debt.[129]

His own sister Amelia, together with her husband Benjamin Broomhall, joined the ranks of the mission at home. Finally, in 1876, Hudson Taylor was on his way back to his beloved China, where a new peace meant the door to evangelization stood open as never before. This was only temporary, but for now the opportunity was there. A convention had been signed at Chefoo on 21 August, enabling the missionaries to travel freely throughout China.

Cheefoo Convention

Officially, the reason for the 1876 treaty was to settle the 'Margery Affair' but the final document dealt with a number of issues not directly related to it. (Augustus Margary was a British diplomat who was murdered by Chinese in 1875). The first part of the treaty covered the resolution of the Affair, demanding the punishment of those implicated in his murder. The second section dealt with official intercourse between the empires and outlined the extraterritorial privileges of British subjects in China. The final part covered trade, outlawing taxes on foreign goods and opening a number of new treaty ports.

(http://history.cultural-china.com).

'Representatives of the CIM were the first and for years almost the only, foreigners to avail themselves of this great opportunity. Far and wide they travelled, penetrating even the eastern Tibet. 30,000 miles were thus traversed in the next eighteen months, Scriptures and tracts being everywhere sold or distributed, and friendly relations almost uninterruptedly maintained.'[130]

It is stiff soil and none but fully consecrated men will accomplish much. Comfort-seeking, etc., won't do there. Cross-loving men are needed . . . There are such openings in China as there never have been and as are not likely to recur. Just while the effect of the Imperial proclamations lasts (and this will largely be over in a very few months) we can do in weeks what would have taken months or years before.[131]

At this time, Hudson Taylor longed for unity amongst the workers. The idea was conceived to organize a conference in Shanghai in May the following year for mutual encouragement.

There were many who opposed his methods and commented upon the fact that most of the missionaries who joined the ranks of CIM were very young and inexperienced, and, therefore, not prepared for such a huge task as the evangelization of the interior of the country. The idea was to bring old missionaries together with the new ones to inspire each other. All missionary societies were invited. In addition to this, he organized a similar conference for Chinese workers, and they, too, gave each other much support.

He came back to England before Christmas 1877, and brought with him a sick mother, a widow, and a few seriously ill children of other missionaries. He began praying for 30 new workers to go out in 1878. With the hope of a larger team came a renewed need for better organization and leadership. 'I have been praying very much this morning for a wise and understanding spirit, and for largeness of heart, and organizing capacity. The Lord makes me equal to increasing claims.'[132]

Great North China Famine

Famine in North China (1876–79) affected an estimated 20 million people. It intensified trafficking and slavery. Many were sold and many died. Hudson Taylor worked hard in England to raise money for the victims and was constantly praying for more missionaries to be sent, mainly women.

Famine and opportunity

Soon after he came home he had to part with his wife again. China was suffering the effects of the Great Famine, especially the northern province of Shanxi. 'By 1879 (after 2 years of drought) when the rains finally fell, the Great North China famine had claimed nine million victims . . . People resorted to eating dried leaves, tree roots, bark, sawdust, dried mud, and even baked pellets of finely ground stone mixed with soil or millet husk – which caused terrible stomach cramps and eventually death.'[133] After much prayer for discernment, Jennie Taylor left for China, leaving the children (two of her own and four from Hudson's previous marriage) in the hands of Amelia Broomhall, who had children also. Jennie was an experienced missionary and could not but respond to the famine-stricken people. She, together with a team of women, threw themselves into hard work straightaway, teaching women to sew and mend things, and later on they used *The Wordless Book* to 'gossip the gospel' while at work. 'The four-colour wordless book had been invented in 1875, as a refinement of Spurgeon's three-colour version, by the American evangelist Dwight

L. Moody, who added the gold page for "the glories of heaven."'[134]

The Wordless Book became a crucial tool for sharing the gospel in China, and it corresponded amazingly well with a similar illustration using colours that had been known there for centuries past. Black represented sin, red was Jesus' sacrifice, white meant our sanctification, and gold pointed to heaven.

Hudson Taylor stayed at home, raising funds, and encouraging all missionaries in the field to take in orphans from the famine affected areas.

In 1878, after an acute attack of malaria, Hudson Taylor accepted an invitation to take a holiday in Switzerland where he slowly recovered.[135] Soon after, due to the help of Benjamin Broomhall (now General Secretary of the Mission) and his wife Amelia (who was looking after 17 children, and missionaries leaving for and returning from China), Hudson Taylor was able to return to China again. Before he set off he visited George Müller and Charles Spurgeon.

However, on the voyage Hudson Taylor became seriously ill. Jennie came a great distance from northern China to meet him in Shanghai and nurtured him back to health. They then departed for the better climate of Chefoo. Experiencing the wonderful climate there, the vision for a sanatorium for missionaries was born. A remarkable course of events enabled Hudson Taylor to buy land and build a sanatorium there. 'After this first sanatorium, or "Judd's house", as it was known for a while, the CIM built a convalescent home, a school for the mission children, a hospital, and a dispensary.'[136]

In 1881, after a good deal of prayer and consideration, Hudson Taylor and his team asked God for 70 more missionaries to come and join them in the field.

Their work was infused with prayer and in everything they looked for God's wisdom. Hudson Taylor believed there were three different ways of working for God.

One is to make the best plans we can, and carry them out to the best of our ability. This may be better than working without plan, but it is by no means the best way of serving our Master. Or, having carefully laid our plans and determined to carry them through, we may ask God to help us, and to prosper us in connection with them. Yet another way of working is to begin with God; to ask His plans, and to offer ourselves to Him to carry out His purposes.[137]

A careful survey of the spiritual work to which we ourselves are called has led us to feel the importance of immediate and large reinforcements, and many of us are daily pleading with God in agreed prayer for forty-two additional men and twenty-eight additional women.[138]

The Cambridge Seven

In 1884 a group of seven wealthy students joined CIM. Among them was the famous English cricket player Charles Studd, better known as C.T. Studd opposite page (back row, left).

After touring Britain and talking about China they set off together for the Far East. They all contributed greatly to the work of God in China. Some died there after life-long service, others later moved on to do amazing things for God in different nations. Their decision catapulted China to a new level of interest in Britain, and many were exposed to its needs because of them. Another who responded was Hudson Taylor's eldest son.

In spite of this, there were delays due to the lack of funding and the low number of applicants. Furthermore, there were troubles at some stations, and throughout it all Hudson Taylor was still not well.

Provisions were on their way though, and some of them came from the most unexpected sources in unexpected ways. Below is a sample gift from a family with a vision for evangelism:

Father	£1000
Mother	£1000
Mary	£200
Rosie	£200
Bertie	£200
Amy	£200
Henry	£200
	£3000

Some time later a similar donation was made: one faithful family generously providing funds for the mission.

John Stevenson

J.W. Stevenson, who had previously served as a missionary in Burma, was appointed Deputy Director of the CIM in 1885. Stevenson proved to be very capable; he, in the same way as Hudson Taylor, always asked for more – and constantly looked for ways in which the mission could grow. After one of his inland journeys he challenged the CIM to ask for a hundred new missionaries to join them in the field. Hudson Taylor quickly caught the vision himself, and the prayer and work for raising up one hundred began. Soon, the hundred flocked to the premises in London.

In 1886, Hudson Taylor and John Stevenson clarified the *Principles and Practice* of the CIM. The book was written for the benefits of the missionaries and future members, and was the fruit of many years of work.

The book said that the relationship of the China Council [established in 1885] to Taylor as General Director, with regard to affairs in China was the same as the London Council's [established 1872] relationship to him with regard to affairs at home. It set out instructions for probationers, the treasurer, the secretary in China, the superintendents, senior and junior missionaries, and women; it spoke about dress, Chinese customs, avoiding offence to the Chinese, and securing rights from mandarins.[139]

Writing in the book about leadership, Hudson Taylor stated:

> The principle of godly rule is a most important one, for it equally affects us all. It is this – the seeking to help, not to lord; to keep from wrong paths and lead into the right paths, for the glory of God and the good of those guided, not for the gratification of the ruler. Such rule always leads the ruler to the Cross, and saves the ruled at the cost of the ruler . . . When the heart is right it loves godly rule, and finds freedom in obedience.[140]

By the end of 1887, 102 missionaries left England for China, from a total of 600 who had applied. The standards were very high. God alone had raised them up, and God alone would provide every penny needed. 'It is not great faith you need, but faith in a great God . . . Let us see to it that we keep God before our eyes; that we walk in His ways, and seek to please and glorify Him in everything, great and small. Depend upon it, God's work, done in God's way, will never lack God's supplies.'[141]

America

God challenged and stretched the vision of the CIM, and the gift of more workers continued – though not in ways Hudson Taylor expected or, even at first, realized. A new opportunity emerged across the Atlantic. Young Henry W. Frost arrived from America to meet with Hudson Taylor, and wanted to discuss the possibility of opening an equivalent of the CIM in America. He left confused and disappointed as Hudson Taylor did not support what he called 'replanting a tree to another soil', but rather preferred to encourage the 'planting' of something more native in form.[142] He did, however, accept an invitation to visit America issued to him (thanks to Frost) by the Conference at Niagara-on-the-Lake, and D.L. Moody. So, in the summer of 1888, Hudson Taylor arrived in the US, with no particular expectations. He travelled there with his son Howard, a young doctor, now aged twenty-five. He stayed until October, and left laden with blessing and good will.

'I think we must have an American branch of the Mission. Do not be surprised if I should bring reinforcements with me' he wrote to Stevenson from there.[143] Soon Hudson Taylor saw the hand of God in his trip, and considered with new openness the possibility of recruiting missionaries. He was deeply moved by the amount of donations after his talks, and started to sense in his heart that the Lord might be leading him to open an American branch of the CIM – but this prospect frightened him.

To have missionaries and no money would be no trouble to me for the Lord is bound to take care of His own. He does not want me to assume His responsibility. But to have money and no missionaries is very serious indeed. And I do not think it will be kind of you dear friends in America to put this burden upon us, and not to send some from among yourselves to use the money. We have the dollars, but where are the people?[144]

Pray especially for guidance in the organization of the work, and for men of calibre to carry it on . . . Abundant spiritual power and some considerable capacity in leadership are just now great desiderata.[145]

He returned to China at peace with the decision to establish the work of the CIM in America. But as soon as he disembarked news came of trouble and death among the team members. 'It was a dark and trying time that winter. There had been so much success, such rapid extension. We were going ahead full sail set, before a favourable breeze. Ballast was needed, though at the time we could not see it, and the prolonged sickness and trial that surrounded us seemed mysterious indeed.'[146]

In addition to all the trials in China, there were those in England who strongly disagreed with the American expansion, and were even ready to resign. This, and a desire to move the headquarters fully to China, were inconceivable to some who were fearful of losing control: even though this move had always been likely, and Hudson Taylor had never hidden his desire to grow local leaders. Some of the members of the London Council were not happy the members of the China Council were invited to revise the *Principles and Practice.*

'Taylor intended the China Council to have executive powers, using the regional superintendents' daily experience of practical problems. However the London Council saw itself as the chief council of the CIM and other councils as subordinate . . . To give major power to the London Council would run counter to a fundamental principle on which Taylor had founded the CIM – direction in China.'[147]

Striving for unity

When the letter containing the London Council's demands reached Shanghai in November 1891 Hudson Taylor felt the mission had reached its gravest crisis to date. '"You have not funds," he told the council, "to support five hundred missionaries; you cannot protect them against an insurrection or in riot; you cannot come out here and administer the affairs of the mission, we must walk before God." As he took up their points one by one, Jennie felt the strain was too much and that it might kill him.'[148]

Everything seemed crowded into those terrible months. I do not know what we should have done without Mr. Taylor, but oh, the look on his face at times!

One thing that deeply touched me at this time was his evident and intense longing to walk upright before God. He would go all lengths to do the right thing and put away misunderstandings. Early spring when our troubles were at their height, he was burdened about the lack of cordiality between ourselves and two former members of the Mission who were still in Shanghai. The trouble had arisen during one of Mr. Taylor's absences in England, but he could not leave it with simply – 'they were wrong, and we did what we could at the time.' He wrote a note saying he would be glad to call upon them and talk matters over, greatly desiring that any bitterness of feeling might be removed. On the 4th March, I remember, he spent a long evening with them, going over the whole story. It must have been very painful, for their attitude was far from conciliatory, but it ended right. He was able to have prayer with them and friendship was restored. Oh, his was a life that stood looking into – searching through and through! Get a man like Mr. Taylor and you could start any mission tomorrow. He walked with God; his life bore the light all through. And he was so gracious and accessible! Day or night, literally at all hours, he was ready to help in sickness or any trouble. For self-denial and practical consecration, one could not but feel, he stood alone.[149]

Because of the strong negative feelings towards the expansion in America, he was forced to travel to England in 1889. He arrived in May, and found God had gone before him in softening the hearts of his opponents, and preparing the way for further growth. Soon Henry W. Frost was appointed secretary and treasurer of the mission in America. Giving up his beautiful home and lifestyle, he and his wife embarked on a journey that would bring thousands of dollars into the mission, and send out hundreds of missionaries to inland China. Furthermore, the work went on growing beyond America, to Sweden and Australia: 'A visit to America in 1888 issued in the formation of the Council for North America, and a similar Council for Australasia was commenced in Melbourne two years later. In the field a China Council was organised in 1886, composed of senior missionaries who meet quarterly in Shanghai.'[150]

In December he published a paper entitled *To Every Creature*, calling for action and united work amongst all the missionary organizations.

The following year Hudson Taylor asked God for a thousand missionaries, and united many different missionary societies and organizations in prayer that God might raise them up in the next five years. Hudson Taylor was raising an army, and soldiers from all denominations and all organizations were to come together in order to reach China with the good news of the gospel. 'Closely associated with the CIM are seven Committees – in England, Norway, Sweden (two), Finland, Germany, and the United States – which send out and support their own missionaries, who in China have the assistance of the educational and other advantages of the CIM, and who work under its direction.'[151]

Pressing onwards and upwards

Darling, I do want our whole life to be an ascending plane – not resting in anything we have learned or felt or attained, but a pressing on end up. God has been faithful to us, as far as we have gone out on His promises and have trusted His faithfulness; but how little we have done so!

What would a great Sovereign think of a proposal to add 100 soldiers in the course of a year to his army of invasion in a country like China? We must get on a higher plane of thought altogether, and of prayer, if we are to walk worthy of God and deal in any sensible way with the world's crying need. Let us ask in faith for such workers from every department as shall be fit and able to deal worthily with their work at home, in America, in China, and for such an enduement of power as shall make the feeblest mighty.[152]

However, not all was going smoothly: the finances were again falling; riots in China against the Catholic Church affected the work of other missionaries and put them in danger; and the continuous conversations with the CIM home office about the nature of their governance were keeping Hudson Taylor in constant prayer. His heart was to release the leadership to the Chinese, rather than governing the mission from distant England, but this was still too radical an idea for those who struggled to keep pace with him.

The Cross Does Not Get Comfortable

Key learning points

Spiritual Formation

Never stop growing spiritually. Hudson Taylor wanted his life to be an ascending plane; both in terms of personal spiritual maturity and fruitfulness in ministry. Developing the former will ensure the latter.

Discerning Vision

Allow God to grow the vision. The first call for missionaries, thirty years previously, had been for five people. Now the call was for a thousand.

Leadership Skills

Seek God's plans. Planning is not in opposition to the work of God, but the best plans are made after God has spoken. Seek him for the vision, and then plan how to get there.

Value character when building a team. Spiritual life and integrity before God are far more important in a person's suitability for ministry than education, wealth, or even gifting.

Partner with others. Having always worked with all denominations, Hudson Taylor now expanded his horizons to open up the CIM to other nationalities, and to partner with other mission organizations. His heart was to encourage unity.

Admit mistakes. Hudson Taylor was willing to admit when he was wrong, for example, in the case of America.

Mission Skills

Keep the message simple. *The Wordless Book* was an excellent tool for the missionaries because its message was simple, and, therefore, easy to convey and remember.

10

To Every Creature

1890–1905

During the last years of his life, Hudson Taylor became ever bolder in asking for more missionaries to join the cause. The response was constant, but he would face more tragedy in these final years than in all the preceding ones.

Pressing on

The vision for raising up a thousand missionaries to China galvanized the CIM, but left them more vulnerable to spiritual attack than before.

If the Spirit of God works mightily, we may be quite sure that the spirit of evil will also be active. When the appeal for a thousand new workers went forth from the Missionary Conference of 1890, the enemy at once began a counter-movement, and riots and massacres have from time to time followed as never before.

The staff of the Mission, in May 1893, consisted of 552 missionaries (including wives and associates). There were also 326 native helpers (95 of whom were unpaid), working as pastors, evangelists, teachers, colporteurs, Bible-women, etc., in 14 different provinces.[153]

By 1895, after the turbulent months of the Japanese War, the number of missionaries was 1,153, most of them women.

An important crisis in China's history has been reached. The war just terminated does not leave her where she was. It will inevitably lead to a still wider opening of the empire and to many new developments. If the Church of Christ does not enter the opening doors, others will, and they may become closed against her. Time is passing. If a thousand men were needed five years ago, they are much more needed now. In view of the new facilities and enlarged claims of China, the next five years should see larger reinforcements than those called for in 1890. Will not the Church arise and take immediate and adequate action to meet the pressing needs of this vast land?[154]

China was humiliated after the war with Japan, and many soldiers who survived returned to their homes poor and frustrated. Discontentment with the ruling power was running extremely high. Meanwhile, Hudson Taylor was working hard on getting the right leadership in place, and making sure the work was not based on him, and would continue after he was gone: 'My aim is to get every part of the work into such a condition that it can be carried on without me, and with this in view I

visit different branches of it in turn. We are specially asking God to give us an increased number of efficient leaders, and to preserve the lives and health of those we
already have.'[155]

Storm clouds gather

There was a storm coming over China, dangerous as
never before, and it would drive out the missionaries and
Chinese workers from all the lands of China. Towards the
close of the century warning signals were present from
time to time. It broke loose in the summer of 1900. The
English, French, Germans, Americans and Russians had
come and claimed much land and property for themselves in the name of trade. The Chinese people were
slowly reaching the end of their patience. Hudson Taylor
soon heard of persecution and killings in many of the
provinces.

Gradually, as 1898 wore on, the outlook with regard to
social and political conditions became increasingly dis-
quieting. While souls were being saved in larger numbers
than ever before and spiritual blessing given, the political
unrest which had been growing since the Japanese war,
and the bitterness of feeling due to the aggressions of foreign powers were hastening a crisis the nature of which
was but too evident. The countermove Mr. Taylor had
anticipated as likely to hinder widespread evangelistic
effort was taking serious form. Too hasty attempts on the
part of the young Emperor to introduce reforms had
thrown the country into a ferment; open discussion in the

European press of the 'partition of China' was goading the authorities to desperation; and the Imperial Government had so lost influence with the people that, as Mr. Taylor wrote in July, there seemed 'little hope of averting a complete collapse.' A powerful rebellion had broken out in Western China in the spring of the year, which was still unsubdued; local uprisings and riots were of frequent occurrence; and finally the Dowager Empress, at the head of the reactionary party, had resumed the reins of government, visiting with dire retribution the over-zealous reformers, and consigning the hapless Emperor to virtual imprisonment in 'the inner apartments.' This had taken place in September, and now in quick succession drastic measures were being taken to reverse the policy of recent years and to curtail the pretensions of foreigners. Needless to say, this sudden change of front on the part of the Government encouraged anti-foreign feeling throughout the country; and as almost the only Europeans in the interior were missionaries, it was against them particularly that hostilities were directed.[156]

The day came when Hudson Taylor learnt of the first martyrdom among the CIM missionaries; he was very ill at that time and was deeply grieved by the news. The loving care of his wife and the grace of God kept him alive.

At the beginning of 1900 Hudson and Jennie Taylor set off for America via Australia and New Zealand. After a busy trip they returned to Europe and settled in Davos, Switzerland. There they were informed of the outcome of the Boxer Rebellion.

In January 1900, before the Boxer outbreak, there were in connection with the Mission, 811 missionaries, including wives and associates; 171 stations; 223 out-stations; 387 chapels; 581 paid native helpers; 193 unpaid native helpers; 8557 communicants in fellowship, 12,964 having been baptized from the commencement. There were 266 organised churches; 788 boarding scholars; 1382 day scholars; 6 hospitals; 18 dispensaries; and 46 opium refuges.[157]

Foreign devils

What made the Boxer Rebellion so powerful, so determined and so merciless? A dire economic situation, droughts that caused lengthy famines, frustrations after years of being yoked and belittled by foreigners, the series of opium wars and unequal treaties, the greed of the western powers stealing and grabbing massive portions of land? All these and more. Foreign business had been conducted at the expense of the Chinese for many years. Anger and crime rose rapidly across Chinese society following the Sino-Japanese war in which China was forced to surrender. Many secret societies emerged in the climate of deep-seated frustration and hatred toward the Japanese, and with that hatred toward all foreigners.

France, Germany, Britain and Russia were gasping for trade opportunities and seizing lands. *I Ho Ch'uan* (Righteous Harmonious Fists), or the Boxer as we now know them, came out of the hardships of this period. For them, foreigners were segregated into three levels (though all of them were considered devils): the first level were the foreigners themselves; then the converts to Christian faith; and then those who worked for them. All deserved to die.

Christian missionaries were a very easy target for Boxers. The hatred of Christians had a long history – they were the authors of misfortunes, some claimed, and because their advent and rise in numbers had coincided with a deterioration in the political and economic conditions in China, they were increasingly the target.[158]

Hudson Taylor, who had recently had a slight stroke, was absent from China at that time, so the heavy burden of responsibility fell upon the shoulders of Mr Stevenson, the Deputy Director in China. He was assisted at Hudson Taylor's request by Mr D.E. Hoste, as well as by other members of the China Council, who had assembled in Shanghai early in July, little conscious of the terrible tragedies then being enacted up-country.

During the terrible year of 1900, when no fewer than 135 missionaries and 53 missionaries' children and many thousands of Chinese Christians were cruelly murdered, the China Inland Mission lost 58 missionaries and 21 children . . . Apart from loss of life, there was an immense amount of Mission property destroyed, and the missionaries were compelled to retire from their stations in most parts of China.[159]

Letter after letter arrived reporting the death of the missionaries and their families. Hudson Taylor was devastated: 'I cannot read; I cannot think; I cannot even pray; but I can trust.'[160]

Indeed, when the worst news was coming, in the middle of August, life seemed to ebb away so fast that he could scarcely cross the room alone, and his pulse fell from seventy or eighty to only forty per minute. Anguish of heart was killing him, and it was only by keeping the tidings back in measure that the slender thread of life held on. With the relief of the Legations and the flight of the Court from Peking (August 14) the Boxer madness began to pass away.[161]

The Boxer Rebellion failed mainly because of the well-trained and united foreign armies. The Boxers were disorganized and many believed that the practice of kung fu protected them from the bullets. After a series of negotiations, a peace protocol was signed in September 1901.

In March 1901, Hudson Taylor had appointed D.E. Hoste as Acting General Director. At that time the issue of compensation for losses during the Boxer Rebellion was being discussed. The CIM had lost a great deal of missionaries, and a lot of stations were badly damaged or totally destroyed. However, it was decided no claims would be made upon the Chinese government, and, even though the losses amounted to thousands of pounds, no compensation would be requested or accepted. In about a year's time many of the stations reopened, and the work among the Chinese began afresh.

The final journey

In July 1903, Jennie Taylor was diagnosed with cancer. Because of its advanced stage there was no hope of treatment. She died on 29 July 1904.

Hudson Taylor was getting ready for his last trip to China in the company of his son and daughter-in-law, Howard and Geraldine Taylor. Arriving in Shanghai in April 1905, he was welcomed by a representative company at the Mission house, for the Spring Council Meetings were in session. Mr Hoste and Mr Stevenson were there, together with some who had come through the worst of the Boxer outbreak, and from the Che-kiang stations Mr Meadows had come up, whose association with Hudson Taylor went back to the old days of the Ningpo Mission.[162]

Dozens of meetings and journeys to visit different stations followed. Travel to the interior was now much easier due to the new railways. In June, he was visiting a mission station in Hunan province.

When the evening meal was ready Mr. Taylor did not feel inclined to come down, and a little later he was preparing to go to rest when his son brought him his supper. While waiting for him to be comfortably settled, his daughter-in-law spent a few minutes alone on the little roof-platform which is such a pleasant addition to many Chang-sha houses.

Twilight had fallen then, and darkness veiled the distant mountains and river. Here and there a few glimmering lights dotted the vast expanse of grey-roofed city. All was silent under the starlit sky. Enjoying the cool and quietness I stood alone awhile, thinking of Father. But oh, how little one realized what was happening even then, or dreamed that in less than one half hour our loved one would be with the Lord! Was the golden gate already swinging back on its hinges? Were the hosts of welcoming angels gathering to receive his spirit? Had the Master

Himself arisen to greet His faithful friend and servant? What was happening, oh, what was happening, even then, over the sleeping city?

Knowing nothing, realising nothing, I went down (says Mrs. Howard Taylor). Dear Father was in bed, the lamp burning on the chair beside him, and he was leaning over it with his pocket-book lying open and the home letters it contained spread out as he loved to have them. I drew the pillow up more comfortably under his head, and sat down on a low chair close beside him. As he said nothing, I began talking a little about the pictures in the Missionary Review lying open on the bed. Howard left the room to fetch something that had been forgotten for supper, and I was just in the middle of a sentence when dear Father turned his head quickly and gave a little gasp. I looked up, thinking he was going to sneeze. But another came, then another! He gave no cry and said no word. He was not choking or distressed for breath. He did not look at me or seem conscious of anything.

I ran to the door and called 'Howard,' but before he could reach the bedside it was evident that the end had come. I ran back to call Dr. Keller, who was just at the foot of the stairs. In less time than it takes to write it he was with us, but only to see dear Father draw his last breath. It was not death – but the glad, swift entry upon life immortal.

'My father, my father, the chariots of Israel and the horsemen thereof!'

And oh, the look of rest and calm that came over the dear face was wonderful! The weight of years seemed to pass away in a few moments. The weary lines vanished. He looked like a child quietly sleeping, and the very room seemed full of unutterable peace.[163]

On 3 June 1905, in Changsha, Hunan, Hudson Taylor, while resting in bed, gently passed into eternal life, with some of his family members and friends around him. He was buried with his first wife Maria, at the foot of the hills near the Yangtze river in Chinkiang.

His life and testimony continue to inspire many today. The China Inland Mission now operates under the name Overseas Mission Fellowship.

'I have found that there are three stages in every great work of God; first it is impossible, then it is difficult, then it is done.'[164]

Endnotes

1. Hudson Taylor in Dr and Mrs Howard Taylor, *Hudson Taylor in Early Years: The Growth of the Soul* (London: Morgan & Scott, 1911), p. 437.
2. M. Scott Peck, *The Road Less Travelled: A New Psychology of Love, Traditional Values and Spiritual Growth* (London: Arrow Books, 1990) p. 24.
3. Howard Taylor, *Hudson Taylor in Early Years*, p. 276.
4. Ibid., p. 65.
5. Ibid., p. 66.
6. Ibid., p. 66.
7. Ibid., p. 70.
8. Ibid., p. 73.
9. Ibid., p. 73.
10. Ibid., p. 72.
11. Hudson Taylor in Howard Taylor, *Hudson Taylor in Early Years*, p. 78.
12. Ibid., p. 79.
13. Ibid., p. 85.
14. Ibid., p. 85.
15. Ibid., p. 101.
16. Ibid., p. 86.
17. Howard Taylor, *Hudson Taylor in Early Years*, p. 88.
18. Hudson Taylor in Howard Taylor, *Hudson Taylor in Early Years*, p. 96.

[19] Ibid., p. 97.

[20] Ibid., p. 86.

[21] Ibid., p. 103.

[22] Dr and Mrs Howard Taylor, *Hudson Taylor and the China Inland Mission: The Growth of a Work of God* (Singapore: OMF, 1988), p. 429.

[23] Ibid., p.107.

[24] Hudson Taylor in Howard Taylor, *Hudson Taylor and the China Inland Mission*, p.118.

[25] Ibid., p. 114.

[26] Ibid., p. 131.

[27] Ibid., p. 123.

[28] Ibid., p. 124.

[29] Ibid., p. 127.

[30] Ibid., p. 141.

[31] Ibid., p. 162.

[32] Ibid., p. 167.

[33] Ibid., p. 167.

[34] R. Steer, *J. Hudson Taylor: A Man in Christ* (Milton Keynes: Authentic Media and OMF, 2005), p. 45.

[35] Hudson Taylor in Howard Taylor, *Hudson Taylor in Early Years*, p. 183.

[36] J. Hudson Taylor, *A Retrospect*, www.gutenberg.org, paragraph 41.

[37] Hudson Taylor in Howard Taylor, *Hudson Taylor in Early Years*, p. 201.

[38] Taylor, *A Retrospect*, paragraph 46.

[39] Hudson Taylor in Howard Taylor, *Hudson Taylor in Early Years*, p. 211.

[40] Ibid., p. 208.

[41] Ibid., p. 215.

[42] Ibid., p. 221.

[43] Ibid., p. 221.

[44] Taylor, *A Retrospect*, paragraph 47.

45 Howard Taylor, *Hudson Taylor in Early Years*, p. 227.
46 Hudson Taylor in Howard Taylor, *Hudson Taylor in Early Years*, p. 229.
47 Ibid., p. 232.
48 Ibid., p. 237.
49 Howard Taylor, *Hudson Taylor in Early Years*, p. 237.
50 Hudson Taylor in Howard Taylor, *Hudson Taylor in Early Years*, p. 249.
51 Taylor, *A Retrospect*, paragraph 48.
52 Hudson Taylor in Howard Taylor, *Hudson Taylor in Early Years*, p. 271.
53 Ibid., p. 271.
54 Ibid., p. 306.
55 Taylor, *A Retrospect*, paragraph 57.
56 Taylor, *A Retrospect*, paragraph 58.
57 Hudson Taylor in Howard Taylor, *Hudson Taylor in Early Years*, p. 371.
58 Ibid., p. 366.
59 Ibid., p. 269.
60 Taylor, *A Retrospect*, paragraph 99.
61 Hudson Taylor in Howard Taylor, *Hudson Taylor in Early Years*, p. 431.
62 Ibid., p. 448.
63 Ibid., p. 437.
64 Taylor, *A Retrospect*, paragraph 109.
65 Howard Taylor, *Hudson Taylor in Early Years*, p. 484.
66 Ibid., p. 497.
67 Ibid., p.500.
68 Marshall Broomhall, *The Jubilee Story of the China Inland Mission* (London: Morgan & Scott, 1866), p. 9.
69 Taylor, *A Retrospect*, paragraph 117.
70 Howard Taylor, *Hudson Taylor and the China Inland Mission*, p. 12.
71 Ibid., p. 12.
72 Broomhall, *The Jubilee Story*, p. 10.

73 Howard Taylor, *Hudson Taylor and the China Inland Mission*, p. 16.
74 Ibid., p. 17.
75 Ibid., p. 30.
76 Taylor, *A Retrospect*, paragraph 120.
77 Howard Taylor, *Hudson Taylor and the China Inland Mission*, p. 31.
78 Ibid., p. 32.
79 Broomhall, *The Jubilee Story*, p. 15.
80 Ibid., p. 15.
81 Ibid., pp. 14–15.
82 Ibid., p. 5.
83 Ibid., p. 6.
84 Ibid., p. 7.
85 Ibid., p. 38.
86 Howard Taylor, *Hudson Taylor and the China Inland Mission*, p. 54.
87 Alvyn Austin, *China's Millions: The China Inland Mission and Late Qing Society, 1832–1905* (Grand Rapids, Michigan: William B. Eerdmans Publishing Company, 2007), p. 112.
88 Broomhall, *The Jubilee Story*, p. 20.
89 Ibid., p. 21.
90 Howard Taylor, *Hudson Taylor and the China Inland Mission*, p. 105.
91 Ibid., p. 118.
92 Ibid., p. 155.
93 Ibid., p. 106.
94 Ibid., p. 107.
95 Ibid., p. 145.
96 Ibid., p. 160.
97 Ibid., p. 162.
98 Ibid., p. 182.
99 Ibid., p. 183.
100 Ibid., p. 183.
101 Hudson Taylor in Howard Taylor, *Hudson Taylor and the China Inland Mission*, p. 166.

[102] Ibid., p. 189.

[103] Ibid., p. 190.

[104] Ibid., p. 191.

[105] Howard Taylor, *Hudson Taylor and the China Inland Mission*, p. 197.

[106] Hudson Taylor in Howard Taylor, *Hudson Taylor and the China Inland Mission*, p. 199.

[107] Ibid., p. 199.

[108] Ibid., p. 200.

[109] Ibid., p. 209.

[110] Ibid., p. 213.

[111] Ibid., p. 217.

[112] Steer, *J. Hudson Taylor*, p. 251.

[113] Howard Taylor, *Hudson Taylor and the China Inland Mission*, p. 228.

[114] Ibid., p. 230.

[115] Steer, *J. Hudson Taylor*, p. 252.

[116] Hudson Taylor in Howard Taylor, *Hudson Taylor and the China Inland Mission*, p. 232.

[117] Ibid., p. 235.

[118] Ibid., p. 236.

[119] Ibid., p. 244.

[120] Ibid., p. 255.

[121] Howard Taylor, *Hudson Taylor and the China Inland Mission*, p. 254.

[122] Hudson Taylor in Howard Taylor, *Hudson Taylor and the China Inland Mission*, p. 256.

[123] Ibid., p. 358.

[124] Howard Taylor, *Hudson Taylor and the China Inland Mission*, p. 266.

[125] Howard Taylor, *Hudson Taylor and the China Inland Mission*, p. 267–68.

[126] ibid., p. 268.

[127] Austin, *China's Millions*, p. 202.

[128] Howard Taylor, *Hudson Taylor and the China Inland Mission*, p. 237.

[129] Ibid., p. 279.

[130] Ibid., p. 285.

[131] Ibid., p. 296.

[132] Ibid., p. 315.

[133] Austin, *China's Millions*, p. 145.

[134] Austin, *China's Millions*, p. 167.

[135] Steer, *J. Hudson Taylor*, p. 270.

[136] Steer, *J. Hudson Taylor*, p. 272.

[137] Hudson Taylor in Howard Taylor, *Hudson Taylor and the China Inland Mission*, p. 355.

[138] Ibid., p. 360.

[139] Steer, *J. Hudson Taylor*, p. 295.

[140] Ibid., p. 296.

[141] Howard Taylor, *Hudson Taylor and the China Inland Mission*, p. 429.

[142] Ibid., p. 438.

[143] Ibid., p. 448.

[144] Ibid., p. 449.

[145] Ibid., p. 365.

[146] Howard Taylor, *Hudson Taylor and the China Inland Mission*, p. 458.

[147] Steer, *J. Hudson Taylor*, p. 326.

[148] Ibid., p. 327.

[149] ibid., p. 462.

[150] Taylor, *A Retrospect*, paragraph 127.

[151] Ibid., paragraph 127.

[152] Howard Taylor, *Hudson Taylor and the China Inland Mission*, p. 467.

[153] Taylor, *A Retrospect*, paragraph 127.

[154] Howard Taylor, *Hudson Taylor and the China Inland Mission*, p. 537.

[155] Ibid., p. 559.

156 Ibid., p. 575.
157 Broomhall, *The Jubilee Story*, p. 129.
158 Victor Purcell, *The Boxer Uprising: A Background Study* (Cambridge: Cambridge University Press, 2010), p. 121.
159 Taylor, *A Retrospect*, paragraph 129.
160 Howard Taylor, *Hudson Taylor and the China Inland Mission*, p. 587.
161 Ibid., p. 590.
162 Ibid., p. 606.
163 Ibid., p. 616.
164 Ibid., p. 276.

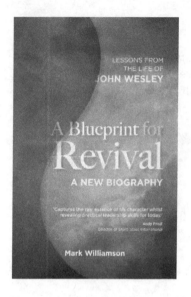

A Blueprint
for
Revival

*Lessons from the Life
of John Wesley*

Mark Williamson

For centuries God has used committed men and women to share his love, lead his people and shape his Church. Whether they feature in the Bible or have been serving God in more recent times we can learn so much from the many leaders and servants who have gone before.

John Wesley was one of the UK's great leaders, whose passion for God led him to do amazing things. *A Blueprint for Revival* clearly lays out the key moments of Wesley's story, using journal extracts, letters and writings to give insight into both the personal and professional aspects of his life. From the influence of his parents to his time at Oxford, from his founding of Methodism to his handling of relationships, this book shows us a man who was dedicated, disciplined and devout.

978-1-85078-962-8